THE KING'S BALLET MASTER

August Bournonville, the grand old man of Danish ballet

THE KING'S BALLET MASTER

A Biography of Denmark's August Bournonville

WALTER TERRY

Illustrated with photographs

Dodd, Mead & Company   New York

PICTURE CREDITS

Fredbjørn Bjørnsson, 5 top, 67, 91, 121
Steven Caras, 148, 149 top
Arnold Eagle, 133
John R. Johnsen, 87 bottom, 130, 131 top, 137, 138 top, 142,
143 top, 150, 151, 152
Ralph McWilliams, 109 bottom, 131 bottom
Myotskov, 88, 132 bottom, 134, 135, 141 left, 143 bottom
Louis Peres, 136
Martha Swope, 125, 126, 127, 128, 138 bottom, 139, 149 bottom
Von Haven Presse, 141 right
Archival prints and photos at the Court Theater Museum were
copied by Niels Elswing

1 2 3 4 5 6 7 8 9 10

Library of Congress Catalog Card Number: 79-55736

ISBN: 0-396-07722-6

For
KIRSTEN RALOV

For twenty-five years the perfect Bournonville dancer and today the loving and learned custodian of one of the great ballet traditions of all time. With my admiration, gratitude and deep affection.

Acknowledgments

I gratefully acknowledge the invaluable assistance of my dear friend and respected colleague, Ebbe Mørk, dance critic of *Politiken*, author, lecturer; Svend Kragh-Jacobsen, dean of Denmark's dance critics; Erik Aschengreen, critic, author, professor of dance; Henrik Lundgren, critic and author; Allan Fridericia, critic-historian; Mrs. Karen Neiiendam and Claus Neiiendam, curators and archivists of the Royal Theater Museum, Christiansborg Castle; Ida Poulsen of the Royal Theater Library, and my absolutely indispensable translator and wonderfully knowledgable research assistant at the Royal Theater Library, Monica Rude; Henning Kronstam, artistic director of the Royal Danish Ballet. And I deeply appreciate the assistance granted me by the Ministry of Culture in Denmark.

August Bournonville as James
in *La Sylphide*

Foreword

It would be presumptuous of me, a non-Dane, to attempt a detailed and definitive biography of a Danish national treasure, August Bournonville. I leave that complex but richly rewarding task to one or more of my Danish colleagues, since each has already done exhaustive and immensely valuable research and reporting on various areas of Bournonville's life and career.

My book, *The King's Ballet Master*, represents the tribute of an American dance writer and a longtime admirer and student of the art of Bournonville on the occasion of the centenary of the death of the great ballet master. Her Majesty Queen Margrethe II, in conferring upon me knighthood in the Order of the Dannebrog, most graciously took note of my many years of worldwide reporting of the accomplishments of the Royal Danish Ballet and, in particular, my service to the Bournonville tradition. This book, I trust, will help extend still further America's, and the English-speaking communities', knowledge of Bournonville in a century that is now discovering that he belongs not only to Denmark but to the world, and that his choreographic art is not a vestige of the nineteenth century but a treasure for all time.

W.T.

Contents

Illustrations

1

A King Is Killed

THE ASSASSINATION of a monarch provided Giuseppe Verdi with the story for one of his greatest operas, *Un Ballo in Maschera* (The Masked Ball), and ultimately provided the Kingdom of Denmark with one of the great ballet masters and choreographers of all time.

Gustavus III of Sweden (1746–1792) was not only a powerful monarch who was able to divest the parliament of its supremacy and restore royal authority, but he was also a cultured man who supported the arts with undiminished vigor. His reign, described as the period of Gustavian Enlightenment, commenced in 1771 and ended abruptly in 1792, when His Majesty was fatally shot by a political discontent while attending a midnight masquerade at the Opera House in Stockholm. But during those enlightened years he nurtured the arts, treasured his artists and became something of a playwright himself. The royal eye was never more astute than when it recognized the exceptional talent of a young French dancer, Antoine Bournonville, and insisted that the extraordinarily handsome and beautifully schooled twenty-one-year-old danseur be engaged for the Opera in the Swedish capital.

The dancer who was to become a royal favorite could boast noble, if not royal, antecedents for himself. The family's history goes back to the Middle Ages, when there were de Bournonvilles in Picardy, with the *de* representing noble position or favored status. There were de Bournonvilles among the officers who fought for the dukes of Burgundy during the raids, forays and wars of the French nobles. And there were artists, too, in the de Bournonville lineage. In the early 1600's,

1

Valentin de Bournonville was organist and choirmaster at Amiens. His son succeeded him in the post and then his grandson, Jacques de Bournonville, who was not only organist and choirmaster but also a distinguished composer of church music. Louis, a brother of Jacques, continued the family's military tradition and died on the battlefield. His son, another Louis, was born with the stuff of theater. He married an actress, Jeanne Evrard, fathered some children, directed the theater at Lyon, deserted his family and disappeared forever.

Louis' daughter, Julia, the eldest, grew up in the world of theater. However, instead of following her mother's profession, she became a dancer. Her career took her to Vienna, where she soon established herself as a major ballerina at the Court Theater. With her position at the Imperial Austrian Court secure, she sent for her two brothers, Théodore and Antoine, in order that they might have the opportunity of studying under the direction of that titan of ballet, Jean-Georges Noverre, choreographer, ballet reformer and inventor of *ballet d'action,* a new concept of the dance art demanding that all movement have dramatic, meaningful content and not simply serve as a showcase of physical prowess.

Théodore died, but Antoine continued his studies in Vienna until he was sixteen. Then he traveled to Kassel, Germany, where his mother was employed in the theater, and it was here he made his debut. His engagement lasted for three years. At nineteen he returned to his native France and, in Paris, continued his career in the company of such illustrious male stars as Auguste Vestris and Pierre Gardel, dancers of his own age. Although Gardel and Vestris outstripped Antoine in matters of international popularity and prestige, both were destined some forty years later to guide another Bournonville, Antoine's son August, to a ballet career that would influence the world of dance forever. Perhaps if Antoine had remained in Paris, the crucible of professional ballet and its undisputed world capital, he might have rivaled Vestris and Gardel. He chose a different course. Admired though he was in both Paris and London, close as he was to such masters as Noverre and the great actor David Garrick, the personal patronage of a king was not to be lightly dismissed.

Mariane Jensen, Danish dancer, the first Mrs. Antoine Bournonville. (She died young.)

Antoine Bournonville (painted by Per Krafft, the elder), August's father. At his Copenhagen debut in 1792 he was described as "a real Apollo."

Lovisa Sundberg, a Swede, the second Mrs. Bournonville and August's mother. At the start, she and Antoine enjoyed what the Danes described as "a Polish marriage."

King Gustavus had seen Antoine Bournonville dance and wanted him for his rejuvenated theater-arts activities in Stockholm. The king and his Danish-born queen supported all of the arts, but Bournonville, from the time of his engagement in Sweden in 1782 until the king's assassination in 1792, was the royal favorite. Even more important, he was the most popular dancer with the public. Among his admirers was Carl Michael Bellman, Sweden's great poet-musician, who took some of Bournonville's French dance airs and improvised upon them, creating songs that were accompanied by zither and even by lute and orchestra.

It was a happy and rewarding life for Antoine, and it seemed he would spend the rest of his days in Stockholm. But then the

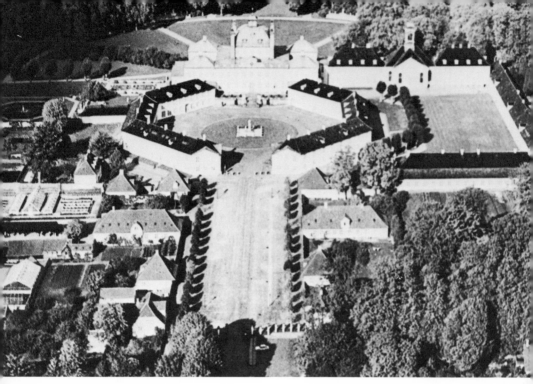

Fredensborg Castle—Summer residence of the Royal Family. The wing (lower right) across the courtyard from the chapel was assigned by the king to Antoine Bournonville as his home. It was here that August was born and raised.

king was killed, the Opera House was closed and, with the shock experienced by the nation and the royal family, there were no immediate signs of what the future would hold for a Frenchman in Stockholm. Bournonville decided to head for Paris.

The trip was to be made by way of Copenhagen, where one of his Stockholm pupils, Carl Dahlen, had made a career for himself as a popular dancer with the Royal Danish Ballet. King Gustavus died March 29, 1792, a few days after being shot at the masked ball. On April 17, Antoine Bournonville made his debut as guest artist with the Royal Ballet in Copenhagen.

For his first performance, Antoine appeared in *Entrée Serieux* and in something described as "an English dance." The critic Thomas Overskou wrote of him: "A real Apollo. He danced with taste, great virtuosity and masculine grace." Further comments appearing in reviews noted that a Mrs. Bjørn was his partner and that in this *Entrée Serieux*, "the beautiful, the assured, the rounded, the light and the soft in all his movements were admired. His English solo he performed with a hearty briskness."

Antoine confirms the fact that his Danish debut was indeed a smash. "I was in dress rehearsal the day of my performance and I was very satisfied with the musical support of my ballets. I danced an *Entrée Serieux* with Mrs. Bjørn and a demi-caractère with Mrs. Jensen. And I dare write that I had the greatest possible success. All the directors, the actors, and the dancers came to my room to kiss me and to compliment me." The kiss that lingered was that of Mariane Jensen. Antoine fell deeply in love with the beautiful twenty-five-year-old dancer who had made her debut at the Royal Theater in 1784 and had developed into a brilliant mime. One critic wrote, "To see her was to love her." Antoine did just that. All his plans for a renewed career in Paris faded away.

Close-up of the first Bournonville home at Fredensborg Castle.

The garden of August's home at Fredensborg.

5

Vincenzo Galeotti (painting, 1816, by Viertel), ballet master and principal choreographer Royal Danish Ballet (1775-1816). His *The Whims of Cupid and of the Ballet Master* (1786) is still in the active repertory of the Royal Danish Ballet and is the oldest ballet extant in its original form.

Anna Margrethe Schall, Denmark's first ballerina of distinction. She danced with Antoine Bournonville in ballets by Galeotti. She also auditioned Hans Christian Andersen when he had dreams . of becoming a ballet dancer!

Antoine and Mariane became engaged almost instantly, for she found herself captivated by this temperamental and remarkably handsome Frenchman. Off he went to Paris to take care of family matters and to see his close colleagues at the Opéra. The Royal Theater in Copenhagen made him a favorable offer and, after some contractual misunderstandings and hitches, an agreement was signed. Antoine Bournonville became a valued member of the Royal Danish Ballet until his retirement in 1823, and a close alumnus of the Danish dance until his death twenty years later. By marrying Mariane in December 1792, he automatically became a Danish subject.

Mariane bore him a son, Antoine, and a daughter. After four years of marriage Mariane died. In due course Antoine "married" his Swedish housekeeper, Louisa Sundberg. Their relationship was what the Danes described as "a Polish marriage"—that is, they were not officially wed. They continued to live in a "Polish" state until Antoine succeeded Vincenzo Galeotti as director of the Royal Ballet in 1816; it was deemed wise that "a public person" should be properly married. Louisa gave him six more children, two boys and four girls. The eldest, Antoine Auguste, was the only one to pursue a dance career—a sister, Charlotte, enjoyed some success as a singer— and was the one to give the ancient name of Bournonville a context that would be known and cherished throughout the theater world.

Together, Antoine senior and his far more famous son, (Antoine) August (the Danish spelling for Auguste), served eleven monarchs as dancers, ballet masters or directors. In France, Antoine had been a junior subject of Louis XV and the doomed Louis XVI; as a child dancer at the Court Theater in Vienna, he had been rewarded by the Empress Maria Theresa, who, delighted with a little dance he had performed, placed a golden chain around his neck. Sweden's Gustavus III had been a very special patron, bringing the Bournonville strain to Scandinavia. Antoine, when he became a Danish citizen, proved to be a loyal subject to his new monarch, Christian VII. In 1801, when the English attacked Copenhagen, Antoine joined the King's Volunteer Guards and fought side by side with his friend, the composer Edouard Dupuy, against the invaders. Years later, in one of his most popular and enduring ballets, *The King's Volunteer Guards at Amager*, August Bournonville used his father's friend, Dupuy, as the hero in a story that had been told by father to son.

Patriotism ran high in 1801. Antoine not only did battle for king and country but also created the role of Regnar Lodbrog in Denmark's first ballet on a Nordic theme, *Lagertha*, with choreography by Galeotti and music of Claus Schall. Mrs. Bjørn was the heroine of this Scandinavian myth, which was modeled after the Greek legend of Jason and Medea. The work itself, like most of Galeotti's ballets, was a pantomime-opera with

7

dances, involving a singing choir as well as corps de ballet. King and commoners reacted enthusiastically to the soaring spirit of a national legend. *Lagertha* premiered January 13, well before the British attack, on the king's birthday. Years later Bournonville wrote, "My father's performance of the legendary hero was absolutely imposing—he himself choreographed quite a bit of his part—and it was performed on the Danish stage for many years. The ballet was praised by the public, and everyone liked the national spirit of this grandiose drama. It was many years before an equal success could supplant *Lagertha*."

Although a loyal subject of his king, Antoine was not without considerable revolutionary spirit. Edgar Colin, the essayist-critic, described him as "a fighter for freedom in the French sense." He was an ardent supporter of the ideals of the French Revolution but was opposed to excesses. On one occasion, however, his enthusiasm carried him almost too far. In the palatial building that is now the Hotel D'Angleterre, he danced a famous French Revolutionary song, not "La Marseillaise" but "Ca Ira," the tune of the *sans culottes*. King Christian was so furious at what he considered antimonarchial expressions —he himself was an absolute monarch—that he let Antoine know he had "nearly danced his way away from the ballet master title" that His Majesty had conferred upon him at Galeotti's death. But Antoine was pro-democratic only in terms of humanitarian ideas, as his son would also be. The Bournonvilles, although they had some close confrontations with their sovereigns, were at all times loyal subjects of not only the absolute monarchs Christian VII, Frederik VI and Christian VIII, too, but also of Denmark's first constitutional king, Frederik VII, and his successor, Christian IX. Indeed, on the occasion of the fiftieth anniversary of August Bournonville's debut, Christian IX honored his old servant and subject, who had "sorely tried" his patience, with the Medal of Merit.

The Bournonvilles, father and son, although revolutionaries in spirit, democratic in tenet and humanitarian in philosophy, served their monarchs faithfully. And one, Sweden's Gustavus III, gave his life unknowingly so that the magic name of Bournonville could belong not to Sweden but to Denmark.

2

"You Will Find Me a Worthy Son"

AUGUST BOURNONVILLE was born in Copenhagen August 21, 1805. If he was not actually born in a trunk backstage, he was most certainly born into the world of theater. As a child it was perfectly natural for him to imitate the actors, the dancers, the musicians who peopled his father's life. And it was inevitable that at eight he would enter the Royal Ballet School at the Court Theater in Christiansborg Castle. Although Danish theater—drama, opera, ballet—dates from 1722 (court ballets, of course, were popular with Danish kings as far back as the late 1500's), it was not until 1771 that the ballet school was established in what is now the enchanting and endlessly fascinating Court Theater Museum.

Ballet classes were available to the Royal Dancers in the 1750's. But the school itself, with graded classes, was established in 1771 under the direction of a French ballet master, Pierre Laurent, a member of a distinguished theatrical family influential throughout Europe. Galeotti came to Copenhagen in 1775 to remain as ballet director and ballet master until his death in 1816. Young August became a pupil not only of old Galeotti but also of his own father, Antoine. In the great tradition of those days, with interlocking arts skills, Antoine played the violin while conducting class, gesticulating with his bow, perhaps using it to touch a recalcitrant leg or a misplaced arm, and then playing the suitable airs as his young charges went through their exercises.

On October 2, 1813, August made his first stage appearance in a bit part as one of the sons of Regnar Lodbrog, a Viking king, in Galeotti's *Lagertha*. This introduction to the profession gave the child "stage fever," as he later recalled. "Screams, noise and slaps seemed to be necessary in school and in rehearsals," he remembered. "Still I saw illusions appealing to my admiring eyes, especially when Galeotti's great tragic ballets were rehearsed and the eighty-year-old master noticed my pleasure and was delighted to see how interested I was despite the fact that the older dancers shouted, 'Look at the boy and see how he makes a fool of himself.' Galeotti, however, liked me very much and gave me several little parts."

The little parts grew into bigger assignments. Less than a year after his debut, he received his first personal applause dancing a Hungarian solo at the Court Theater. This was not the home of the Royal Ballet, which performed at the Royal Theater (built in 1748) in Kongens Nytorv, but the headquarters for the school, and a place for occasional performances as it remains to this day. One of August's first fans was a little girl his age but from a more important family. She was Princess Wilhelmina Maria, who came often to the performances and asked—"commanded" would be too strong a word for one so young!—that "the little Bournonville would please appear." As he danced his Hungarian solo, the audience murmured, "He's just like his father."

The stage fever was so hot that August could think of nothing but the theater. He danced all morning, went to school for a while in the afternoon and, of course, learned French at home. He was a voracious reader, and years later he described himself as self-educated through reading, learning his "life's philosophy" from Holberg's epic poem, *Niels Klim's Subterranean Journey* and acquainting himself with his Scandinavian heritage through the Norse dramas of Oehlenschäger. Not all was dancing for this multitalented child. He was taught declamation by one of the great Danish actors, Michael Rosing; on Rosing's death, he continued his acting studies with Lindgreen and Frydensdahl, both prominent actors. Such training was almost standard, for Galeotti ballets, as were others of that and the preceding period, employed mime as

August Bournonville, the still youthful director of the Royal Danish Ballet.

much as, and perhaps more than, dance movement. His father's first wife, noted as a dance mime, spent the final four years of her short life as an actress.

Thus August had roles in plays as well as in ballets. He also had an ear for music and sang in a beautiful boy soprano voice. These talents were combined October 29, 1817, when twelve-year-old August played the part of Adonia in a music-drama, *Solomon's Judgment*, and sang a romance called "The Mother with Her Drooping Wings." The occasion for the performance was the queen's birthday, and such was the impact of his rendition that the great burst of applause that greeted him originated in the royal box.

His instruction was expanded to include violin lessons under the orchestra conductor, Wexschall, and once again he displayed amazing talent in yet another area of the performing arts. Antoine and his colleagues wondered, and discussed, what direction this gifted child would take. At this point it was "stage" fever, not "ballet" fever exclusively, that had infected the boy.

The future of August Bournonville was determined, probably inadvertently, by the king. Antoine had applied for a study grant from *Ad Usus Publicus*, a Danish foundation governed by the sovereign, to go to Paris for study. As one of three directors of dance since Galeotti's death in 1816, it was important for him to keep abreast of the newest trends in ballet, and trends were set by Paris. He received permission to take his son with him for the summer and fall of 1820. The royal grant was specifically for ballet study. Still, the climate of Paris was such that all of the performing arts activities appealed to the youth. Rossini, the composer, heard August sing and strongly recommended to Antoine that his son study to become an opera singer. The violin continued to bring him joy; in later years he would take great pleasure playing with string ensembles composed of members of the Royal Orchestra.

The comparatively brief stay in Paris—including the long travel time, it ran from late March to December—exposed the young artist, who turned fifteen during his stay, to a dazzling new world of theater. Although he actually took class with only his father, he watched in action such illustrious teachers as Maze and Vestris (the younger Vestris, Auguste, whose equally famous father, Gaetan, was hailed as God of the Dance). The male dancer was still paramount, but it was his twilight, for the classical age of ballet, more than a century old, was about to give way to the new Romantic Age with its dancing on *pointe*, the supremacy of the ballerina and the disappearance of opera-ballet-pantomimes. It was a marvelous age in which to live, especially for one so young, so very talented and so eager to absorb the artistic, intellectual, academic and revolutionary riches afforded him. Indeed, August Bournonville, destined to be a major and lasting force in the Age of Romantic Ballet, would also be the only preserver of the glittering age of the Vestrises, who themselves represented the culmination of a ballet vision that the Sun King himself, Louis XIV, monarch and dancer, had shaped into institutional form as the seventeenth century drew to a close.

In Paris, August was discovering that the ballets of Galeotti, so much admired when he was a little boy and vehicles for his own first performances, suddenly seemed as old as their protagonists. He had been only six years old when Galeotti, then

Decor (by Chipart) for Galeotti's *Lagertha* (1801), the first ballet
created on a Nordic theme.

nearing eighty, had produced the ballet of *Romeo and Juliet*.
It proved to be very popular, almost as successful as *Lagertha*,
but looking back on it from a maturer viewpoint, he realized
that everything about it was an echo from the past. His own
father, at fifty-one, was playing Romeo. The Juliet was close
to forty, Paris was forty-three and Galeotti himself, at seventy-
eight, was Friar Lawrence (Lorenzo). Also in this year of
1811, the treatment of the theme belonged to a disappearing
concept of ballet, for Galeotti included solo songs as well as
solo dances in his production, there was a chorus as well as a
corps and the key conflict of the feud between Capulets and
Montagus was obscure. Bournonville realized that the ballet's
plot resembled Striebelt's opera of *Romeo and Juliet* far more
than it mirrored the course of the Shakespeare drama. At
seventy-eight, Galeotti was choreographing exactly as he had
when he created his first ballet at twenty-six, adhering to the
principles established by his mentors, such as Angiolini
(Noverre's rival), Canziani, Viganò, Gioia.

The 1820 visit to Paris, although a revelation, was too short. August had to go back, but first there would be three more years of growing up in Copenhagen. He became a member of the Royal Theater assigned to a repertory that became less and less interesting and challenging to him. His father, now past sixty, was still performing, but he was meant to be neither a director nor a choreographer. The Royal Ballet, faltering during Galeotti's declining years, went into a sharp decline during the decade and a half that Antoine strove to guide it.

Denmark was in a bad way economically. War had left the kingdom unsettled. In 1813 the country had gone bankrupt; Antoine had lost all his money. The only bright spot was that his pension was honored by giving him and his family a rent-free home in Fredensborg Castle, the monarch's summer home some distance from Copenhagen. The Bournonvilles lived in a distant wing of the sprawling, beautiful castle, and Fredensborg was to remain a family center and a refuge from city pressures for three generations of Bournonvilles.

At nineteen, August convinced his king that he should return to Paris for a brief period of study and coaching and to take his dance examination at the Opéra. To pass this test in the world's ballet capital would give him an international prestige unobtainable in the provincial capital of his homeland. Copenhagen was an overgrown town of some 80,000 people, but Paris! Ah, Paris was a city of 120,000 sophisticates! Frederik VI was the real boss of the Royal Theater, and although Frederik Conrad von Holstein, who had created le Corps des Chasseurs du Roi (the inspiration for Bournonville's *The King's Volunteer Guards on Amager*), was the chamberlain in charge of the theater, the king took his own role most seriously. He gave careful thought to the request of his talented young subject and granted him permission to leave for Paris, while retaining his salary, for the period essential for his final studies and examination. At the time, he did not know that he had a rebel on his hands, loyal but disobedient.

August left Copenhagen as a solo dancer in the spring of 1824. He had permission to remain in Paris for one year and three months, the period sufficient to prepare for and, he hoped, pass his examinations. The fifteen months, however,

14

were to stretch into five years, during which Danish ballet would go into a near-disastrous decline while the young Dane who was to bring it to its peak of accomplishment was preparing for the task.

August, who had studied with only his father during his 1820 visit to Paris but who had watched the teaching of Gardel and Vestris, now wanted Gardel to be his instructor. Gardel, however, was not available for teaching at that time. He suggested that the young Dane work under the supervision

Pierre Jean Laurent (The Younger) (1759-1831), pupil of the great ballet master-choreographer-innovator, Jean-Georges Noverre, and Denmark's first major ballet master.

of Vestris. At first August accepted this second choice grudgingly, but he came to admire Vestris, his style, his school and his classicism in addition to his unequaled knowledge of dancing for the male. Reports on August's programs and progress, as well as descriptions of his studies, are contained in his voluminous correspondence with his father.

The trip to Paris, by way of Kiel, Hamburg and Brussels, took thirteen days. Immediately he found lodgings forty steps "more or less" from the Opéra for forty francs per month. He described his quarters as "a very pretty bedroom" with a closet, a toilet, an alcove for the bed and "mahogany furniture." Within an hour of his arrival, he was discovered by his father's

Auguste Vestris, son of Gaetan Vestris (described as the God of the Dance) and one of the great male dancers in ballet history—Antoine's colleague and contemporary and August's principal teacher.

old friend Louis Nivelon, who immediately took him under his wing and treated him partly as a friend and partly as a son. August had no time for homesickness, for he dined with Nivelon, friends and family and "with my feeble talents have sung, played the violin and also the piano! Nivelon has presented me to society as a brave Danish boy, the son of his best friend and his adopted son."

Gardel was equally affectionate and helpful to him as the son "of an old friend for whom he had deep attachment." Although his own dance studio no longer existed, he had personally recommended August to Vestris for training in those ballet areas he needed most—"balance, pirouettes and arms." Vestris accepted August as a pupil for sixty francs a month. At the first class, he was asked to show Vestris what he could do. August wrote to his father that the great dancer was "astonished" to see that his technique and schooling were so good. A one-hour private lesson starting at eight in the morning was followed by two hours with a young lady of greater technical accomplishment, thus challenging his own degree of prowess.

Everyone treated him as if he were a very special person, dear to them because of his father but also of concern because of his instantly recognizable gifts. "Nivelon has deposited my money and I have the receipt," he wrote his father. Also, "I am extremely satisfied with my lessons with Mr. Vestris and what is more, he is very pleased with my zeal, my diligence and my instant willingness. He is very exact about the lessons and comes to class three times a week at eight in the morning and three times at nine and remains until eleven. I get up every morning at six and always arrive one half hour before the lesson so that I'm absolutely prepared when Vestris arrives. He has taken me in friendship and cultivated my talent with extreme care, he rigorously points out my faults but treats me with consideration."

Vestris found, for example, that the placement of his student's arms was quite correct but recommended that they be "more rounded" when moved to "second position" and that they be held at "equal height." No details were overlooked. After classes with Vestris, August would practice by himself each afternoon from three to four and a half hours. He learned to be not only diligent but patient and to obey every instruction, no matter how minor it seemed, that Vestris gave him. His discovery of a new self caused him to write a letter to his father in which he said that in retrospect he could now benefit from the "precious lessons" Antoine had given a headstrong youth. With pride, but with an irresistible touch of contriteness, he wrote, "You will find in me a worthy son of an excellent [ballet] master and a worthy son of an excellent father."

In addition to his arduous dance schedule, he managed to continue his violin practice, warmly encouraged by the composer Cherubini. Ballerinas, ballet masters, musicians offered the young Dane both encouragement and friendship. He was regarded as a protégé of Gardel and he was a pupil of Vestris; Nivelon watched out for his money and Mme. Gardel mothered him. No eager, ambitious ballet student could have asked for finer auspices than August Bournonville received. Day by day he met and came to know the greatest figures in the world of ballet, opera and instrumental music. He was in Paris for the death of a king, Louis XVIII, brother of the guillotined Louis XVI, who had headed the royalist Restoration, and he was present when his successor, Charles X, was welcomed with a review of 40,000 men in the Champs de Mars. But with all this regal display, August did not fail to make mention that the choreographer Filippo Taglioni had arrived in Paris with his family and that people were saying that Taglioni's daughter was very good-looking and had started work at the studio of one of the most famous teachers in Paris, Jean-François Coulon. August had no way of knowing that Marie Taglioni, a year older than himself, was destined to change the course of ballet forever and, as the protagonist of her father's ballet, *La Sylphide*, to usher in the Romantic Age of Ballet in 1832 and to make dancing on *pointe*, theretofore limited in use as optional, an essential for all ballerinas.

In 1824, Paris had yet to fall completely under the spell of Marie Taglioni. The Swedish-born dancer had made an auspicious debut in Vienna in 1822 in one of her father's ballets (*La Réception d'une Jeune Nymphe à la Cour de Terpsichore* —a prophetic title!) and had been carefully groomed by him for a great future while he fulfilled duties in Munich and Stuttgart. When August first saw Marie in 1824, her Paris debut was still three years away and her triumph was eight years into the future. For August, the important Taglioni was the father, a friend of his own father, Antoine. But the mere mention of key dance names in simple letters written by a boy to his father gives the clue to a momentous change, for here were Vestris and Gardel, the titans of an era about to fade into history, and Taglioni, the herald and symbol-to-be of a new era. Quite unaware of it, August Bournonville at nineteen was enviably poised on a new frontier, with the accumulated riches of the great ballet past behind him and the promise of an incredible golden age of dance ahead.

For the moment, however, August was concerned about his future financial status. Like all boys away from home for the first time, he found that he had to write to "Cher Papa" for some extra money. Leading up to his request, he provided Antoine with the detailed budget he had prepared for himself. Each month it cost him sixty francs for lessons with Vestris and sixty francs for thirty dinners. He wore out six pairs of shoes, at a total of fifteen francs, and drank sixteen francs worth of wine (eight bottles). He listed butter, sugar, bread, coffee, laundry. Apparently his father had told him that he

Center, August Bournonville's costume worn in entrées choreographed by his father, Antoine (1822-1823). On the chair, his costume for *The New Penelope*. These rare costumes are on display at the Court Theater Museum, Christiansborg Castle, Copenhagen.

was spending too much for his dinners (two francs each), but he assured his father that what he ate was absolutely necessary, that "neither the quality nor the quantity are [sic] more than I need." But he did need more money than he had planned, and so he told his father that without in any way abusing his generosity he would like further assistance from home for the one whom Vestris was now describing as "the jewel of his classes." Presumably papa sighed and complied as do most fathers.

Nearly two years passed before August was given his examinations, his finals, by the judges at the Opéra. He had stayed in Paris past the time granted him by King Frederik, but his excuse was valid: illness (a bout with rheumatic fever) had interrupted his studies. During those years, guided, influenced, instructed and exposed to the most exalted company of artists in the western world, he had learned and he had observed. His quest for knowledge was avaricious, but he was not blinded by the company he kept—he had his own ideas. He saw in rehearsal, and even in class, the last efforts of one of the great ballerinas of the day, Fanny Bias, an early

19

and successful exponent of *pointe* dancing. He studied assidu-
ously the classical ballet school as given him by Vestris and
noted that the training, based on the tenets of Vestris-père
(the great Gaetan of an earlier era) and Dauberval, was the
best preparation for a new era of ballet and that the student
should avoid those superficial innovators, those pretenders
who would discard some of the firmly established principles
of technique and style inherited from the past. Yet he was not
blind to progress and found himself impatient with old-
fashioned ballets, slow of pace, dated in structure, boring to
him. Those ballets were inextricably bound up with tiresome,
stilted operas.

Of paramount importance to him was the examination. In
a letter to Antoine dated March 10, 1826, he began with a
headline: "EXAMEN—TRIOMPHE DEBUTS!!!!" This "motto"
he tells his "dear & good Papa" was planned to paint a picture
of the "joy which took possession of my soul this day, a day
which marks an epoch in my life. Praise be to the bountiful
God who has blessed twenty-two months of painful work. This
morning at eleven o'clock I passed this solemn examination
before the Administration and the Committee of Artists as well
as a crowd of friendly spectators." An hour after the examination, Gardel returned to say that the judges had voted unani-
mously to pass the aspirant and to praise not only his
deportment but also his aptitude for work. Gardel added that
August Bournonville "would go far."

Two months had elapsed between August's letter home
describing his triumph and his preceding report. Apologizing
profusely for his unfilial neglect, he explained that preparing
for his examination had filled every second, that Vestris and
Gardel had pointed out areas of technique that needed cor-
recting and that increased practice was essential. Finally, he
noted that an examination was one hundred thousand times
more intimidating than a theater debut.

Shortly after his examination, August Bournonville made
his debut at the Paris Opéra. His first appearance was April 5
in a pas de deux with the ballerina Lise Noblet and in a pas
de trois from *Nina*, a ballet he knew well, although in a different version by Denmark's Galeotti. His second appearance was

in François Albert's *La Lampe Merveilleuse*, in which he danced a pas de trois with Mme. Noblet and a Mme. Lacroix. Subsequently the role of Zéphire in the ballet *Zéphire et Psiché* (Psyche) earned him great applause. But a special favorite from the start was a new pas de deux created by Vestris, which he danced with Noblet as a divertissement.

It was a time of heady happiness for August. He missed his family deeply and he never thought of himself as anything but a loyal Dane, but he did *not* want to return to Copenhagen. The administration of the Royal Theater ordered him to return. Popular opinion was that Danish public money had paid for his ballet education and that he did indeed belong to Denmark. His demands for returning seemed outrageous to the budget-minded direction of the Royal Theater, so much so that he was told that they did not dare show his letter to the king. August, however, bypassed them and wrote directly to King Frederik. His letter of apology for not returning to Copenhagen was accepted by the king, who not only forgave him but ordered the directors of the Royal Theater to offer August the same post and the same pay he had had before he left.

It was clear that if Danish ballet were to survive it would need the talents of young August, whose successes in Paris were swiftly reported to the Danish capital. His promotion to soloist status in the ballet world's most celebrated company made him even more valuable. August, young as he was, knew that he must bargain then and later for what he deemed best for himself and for the ballet he served with such "strength" and "grace," as the French had pointed out. When August turned down the king's offer, he did so not only because he wanted more money and a better position and because a season in London, as second male lead with a group from the Opéra, was projected, but he knew that if he was to be anything more than a dancer with the Royal Danish Ballet, he would have to be invested with some real authority. The directors, desperate to have him, were willing to negotiate. This time the king stepped in and refused to elevate August to a higher post. His Majesty stated, "We find that Bournonville's demands are so exaggerated that we do not want the direction to negotiate."

Bournonville remained in Paris, building his reputation, adding new roles to his repertory, living a life in company with the foremost artists of his time. But pleasures and praise did not spoil him. His love was for his art. The librettist Adolphe Nourrit, who was to write the book for *La Sylphide,* said of him, "That little devil, even if the theater was burning over his head, would not leave the stage until he had finished his last dance and his last entrechat!"

3

Troubles:
Court, Courtship

IN THE WINTER of 1827–1828, August Bournonville, twenty-two and a soloist with the Opéra in Paris, made his first appearance as a guest artist and fell in love, presumably seriously, for the first time. In Paris he had seen Shakespeare plays performed in English by English actors, and the impact of the tragedies, the comedies, the poetry and, indeed, the very dramatic structure of the plays most certainly influenced his own choreography in the years ahead. He learned the English tongue in a matter of six weeks, possibly in order to savor Shakespeare more fully, probably to prepare for his first London engagement in January 1828, and certainly to communicate more perfectly with the seventeen-year-old Louisa Court, an English dancer known as Mlle. Louise, who had come to Paris to study with Maze, one of the most popular teachers at the Opéra. August fell madly in love with her, and the wooing could have asked for nothing better than that he would be traveling with her to London and performing with her. He had been engaged for the tour by M. Anatole (Anatole Petit), a soloist with the Opéra, to join a French ballet group starring, in the male contingent, François Albert, who already had a devoted London following.

The courtship had begun in Paris when August was rehearsing for the tour with Louisa, and it continued as they traveled by stagecoach from Paris to Calais and England, interrupted only by the channel crossing that made August so seasick—"as sick as a dog"—that thoughts of love disappeared. They returned as he recovered, and his romantic hopes were supported by the warmth with which Louisa's mother and stepfather received him in their home. He was thanked for his care in attending to their daughter during the long journey from Paris, and the Courts found him lodgings that were not only close to the King's Theatre, Haymarket, where the French ballet group was performing, but also close to their home.

It was not long before August sensed that the older Courts were more devoted to him than was Louisa. While the troupe was journeying in the same coaches from Paris to its final London destination, one member, Caroline Brocard, was traveling alone with her mother in a luxurious coach provided by an admirer-protector. This seemingly unimportant fact omened Louisa's decision about August's ardent suit. When he proposed to her, offering her a modest artist's home and a one-horse vehicle, she turned to him with scorn and, for her dismissal, said, "No, no, I want a carriage!"

His romantic state of mind rose and fell like a fever chart. "I did not need many weeks to be completely convinced," he wrote, "that my rising passion met no response." But he continued hopeful, and when she wished to attend a chic soirée and was told by her stepfather that she could go only if escorted, and presumably watched, by young Bournonville, she treated him with renewed warmth. At the party he soon discovered that he was merely a cover for a continuing flirtation with a young officer. Yet he said, "My obsession has taken violent dimensions, I tossed on rising and falling waves of hope and despair. . . ." He even attended fencing classes so that if a serious rival should emerge, he would be prepared "to run my sword through him."

Although August was as violently lovesick as he had been seasick, it did not interfere with his dancing nor with his dedication to his career. On opening night at the King's Theatre, January 12, 1828, he had danced in Anatole's new ballet, *Hassan et le Calife,* on the same bill with Meyerbeer's opera, *Margherita d'Anjou.* He and Eugénie LeComte (a ballerina from Bordeaux), the two newcomers to the London stage, were described as "agreeable additions" to the otherwise familiar ensemble and were "well received." Bournonville himself noted that he got "unanimous applause." His greatest London success came with the third ballet bill, which featured Anatole's *Le Sicilien, ou l'Amour Peintre,* in which he and his Louisa shared a triumph. Their tarantella was enthusiastically received and even encored, and Bournonville wrote his mother that "it is very exhausting to dance it twice."

Louisa's offstage rejections of his romantic attentions and aspirations left him in dark despair: "My castles in the air had now fallen in ruins, but the flames still raged and the storm in my young breast threatened to destroy my health." As the three months in London came to a close, his employer and ballet master, Anatole, took him aside and talked to him sternly and in fatherly fashion about the foolishness of unrequited love. When he took his leave of the Courts, he said an affectionate farewell to the family and merely shook hands with Louisa. A few days later, after another rough channel crossing and a bout with seasickness that left him "half dead," he landed in France and found that in a few short hours he had recovered from both sicknesses, of the sea and of the soul. "The feverish dream" was over, and the young dancer awoke "sound and well."

The paths of August and Louisa crossed twice again, once in Bordeaux where he missed seeing her but visited with her mother and noticed a baby in a cradle. But there was no sign of the "magnificence and wealth" of which she had dreamed. The second occasion was in 1861 and she seemed like an old lady. Her daughter, now grown up and an aspiring London actress, was introduced to an "old friend" by Louisa, and the girl informed him that she planned "to marry a rich man." Perhaps she did, or perhaps, like her mother, she would settle for hard work and a long and modestly successful career.

August, on his return to Paris, did not dwell for long on the affairs of the heart in London. He had enjoyed visiting with his father's old friends, the Noverres, who had made London their home after the death of the great Jean-Georges, for the widow spoke only English and the city where Antoine had danced briefly in Noverre's London-based French company was her home. August had attended the English theater every night that he himself was not performing and had been fascinated with English stagecraft. He also approved the habit of British performers who drank no wine on the day of performance but made excellent tea. English beer? He found it heavy and not good for his *"légèreté."* Finally, of London he wrote, "I was well received, well applauded and *well paid."*

Now began the intensified exchange of letters between August and the administration of the Royal Theater in Copenhagen. The directors accused him not only of excessive demands but of pretentions far greater than those ever displayed by the most esteemed artists of the Royal Theater. August responded, not in so many words to the administration but in explanations to his father, that he would not return to Copenhagen and receive the equivalent of "alms." In a sharp letter he retorted that even if he were not considered to be as estimable as the Danish dancers at home, that he had high ideals and plans for his own future and that he would have felt joyful if he could have had an opportunity to "improve the lot" of his Danish dancing comrades. However, if his demands seemed exaggerated, he would offer his formal resignation. His leave, of course, was long since over and he was in disfavor with king and administration, but he had not been dismissed as a member of the Royal Danish Ballet nor had he ever before actually threatened to resign.

August was in something of a quandary. He had been paid handsomely for his London season. And as a soloist at the Paris Opéra, his opportunities for greater rank and greater pay seemed certain. Furthermore, he was invited to Vienna at a generous stipend, and Berlin topped that offer. August Bournonville liked money. He wanted it for himself but, more than that, he wanted fair pay for his dancers and honorable treatment for them, a policy he pursued throughout his long career as he fought to have the dancer treated with the same regard as an actor or opera star.

In the fall of 1829 he returned to Copenhagen to visit his family and, as it turned out, to make guest appearances with the Royal Ballet. The direction felt it would be wise for king and public to see for themselves how valuable August could be to them. The company was in a bad way. Antoine had retired as a director in 1823 and retreated to his beloved home in the wing of Fredensborg Castle. Following Galeotti's death, Antoine had shared a triumvirate direction with his pupils Pierre Larcher and Paul Funck from 1816 to 1830, and their regime saw the Royal Danish Ballet at a low ebb.

Before August made his guest appearances at the Royal Theater, he was expected to report to the king. He did so, but with considerable trepidation, for he had disobeyed his sovereign by remaining in Paris long past the period granted and he had refused to accept the offers of the king's administrators at the Royal Theater. "I went to the king," he reported. "He did not advance toward me as he usually did but stood and leaned against a table in the middle of the room.

"I started with a prepared sentence on such subjects as devotion and love of the fatherland. 'Very well,' interrupted the king, 'but *you* have stayed away.' A little astonished, I dared to say that no one seemed to want me very much at the Royal Theater. 'Rubbish!' said the king. 'Who said that we don't want you at home?'" And then young August displayed his diplomacy coupled with stubbornness, a combination that characterized most of his confrontations with his kings. "But, Your Majesty, I was much too young to take over a leading position. And an inferior position would have spoiled my little bit of talent."

Whether King Frederik was taken in by this shrewd doubletalk would be hard to say, but he was at least mollified: "Very well. I quite understand you prefer the Opéra in Paris to the theater in Copenhagen. But we cannot give you that much money."

"I pray, Your Majesty," replied August, "to be convinced that I would do everything to put my powers at the service of Your Majesty."

"Well," said the king, "let us see what you can do. Everyone maintains that you have made the most astonishing progress."

"Your Majesty is no longer angry with me?"

"No, not at all. I will see you at the gala performance. Go with God."

On September 1, 1829, August returned to his home theater

to appear in dances from *La Somnambule;* his own ballet, *Celebration of the Graces;* and *The Soldier and the Peasant,* also created by him. (*Somnambule,* choreographed by Aumer, was staged in Copenhagen by Bournonville.) Some members of the audience laughed at what they regarded as newfangled choreography, a vast change from the old operatic-style ballets of Galeotti that represented the only kind of ballet most of them had ever seen. But there was no argument about his dancing. The audience screamed its approval with, "He flies! He flies!" The reviews were excellent. A poet wrote of his performance in *Somnambule:* "He speaks during his mime, he soars in his dances." As for the king, he was heard to exclaim more than once, "Charmant! Charmant! Now that's what I call dancing!"

After three months of guest appearances, it was apparent to the theater directors and administrators that they absolutely must have August Bournonville with them permanently. Negotiations recommenced immediately. This time he was offered the posts of principal dancer, director of the ballet (not ballet master as yet of the Royal Ballet but only as court ballet master) and chief choreographer. It was everything he had wanted except for the pay, which was far less than Vienna and Berlin had offered and much, much less than he could earn in theater engagements in Italy and England. He refused the contract.

Dutifully he reported to the king, who simply said to him, "Little Bournonville, it is settled now. I wish you a happy journey, but don't forget how you treated your master and your king."

Sadly Bournonville withdrew. As he was about to depart for Paris, the entire situation suddenly became clear to him. He was actually stepping into his carriage when he knew, and irrevocably, that he had made the wrong decision, that he had asked for too much money and given money an importance that, in the total view of his artistic future, it did not warrant. He delayed his departure, signed the contract and returned to Paris to fulfill his final commitments, to pack his belongings and to return to Denmark, where every opportunity existed to become one of the great dance masters of all time.

4

The King's Prodigal Returns

AUGUST BOURNONVILLE'S return to Copenhagen saved the Royal Ballet. In chronicles of that period, the word "saved" is recurrent. Probably the Royal Ballet would not have disappeared but would have become simply an opera ballet troupe appearing, where needed (or tolerated), in operas and lyric dramas. As a dancer, August electrified the Danish public in such ballets as *Paul et Virginie,* a work based on a Gardel ballet; *La Somnambule* (the Aumer ballet staged by Bournonville) and *Soldier and Peasant.*

A vivid memory of his return was that of the great Danish actress-dancer Johanne Luise Heiberg: "Bournonville moved me with his perfect dancing and his strange and moving mime expression. The scene in the last act [*La Somnambule*] when he has to give up his wedding and he cries, this scene belongs to the most beautiful I have seen on our stage. I have a born sense of beauty and plastique has always had a great attraction for me. My heart just jumped when I saw these ballets and I sighed that I did not belong to the ballet any more. To stay home on a night when the ballet was on was almost impossible for me."

Bournonville and Mme. Heiberg were good friends, as were Bournonville and the actress's husband, Johann Ludvig Heiberg, until the latter became director of the Royal Theater and quarreled with Bournonville over the degree of prominence ballet should have. Johanne Luise Heiberg (born Pätges) pursued a career that is worth reviewing in some detail, for it incorporated talents, experiences and backgrounds uniquely characteristic of Danish theater, particularly with respect to the overlapping, even the integrating, of dance and drama in the masterworks of Bournonville. It must be remembered that Bournonville himself could just as easily, in terms of talent and opportunity, have found his place in ballet, drama, symphony or opera. In addition, it is important to bear in mind that his chief sources of inspiration were the ordinary people, be they in Denmark, Italy or Russia. Further, he would discern and engage talent not only from royal classrooms and theaters but from popular centers of entertainment. Johanne herself got her start in the public Deer Park on the outskirts of Copenhagen.

She was born in Copenhagen in 1812 of refugee parents from Germany, her father a Catholic from the Rhineland and her mother a Jewess from Frankfurt. There were nine children supported chiefly by the mother, for the father was a dreamer who had little success with the bars he attempted to run in Copenhagen. Eventually his wife opened a refreshment stand in Deer Park and here, in summer, tea and pancakes were served in the tent that was their establishment. Nearby lived an artist who was popularly known as The Jew Under the Tree. The artist's daughter befriended Johanne, was charmed by her instinctive bursts of dancing and playacting and urged her mother to take her to the ballet school at the Court Theater for an audition. The child was accepted and had as her first teacher Pierre Larcher, one of the directors of the Royal Ballet. She progressed rapidly in ballet and, like Bournonville also as a child, displayed multitalents.

She was given a few little acting parts. On February 12, 1826, when she was only fourteen, she played a role in a vaudeville sketch at the Court Theater so successfully that Johann Ludvig Heiberg, present in the audience, believed that he had discovered an immense new acting talent. The immensely gifted Mr. Heiberg began to write parts for her, his interest became love and at his urging she left the ballet at the Court Theater and enrolled at the Royal Theater as a drama pupil.

August Bournonville and Andrea Kraetzmer in the title roles in
Paul et Virginie (a ballet based on a famous one choreographed by
the French star, Pierre Gardel).

In the best tradition of great romances, Heiberg proposed to Johanne through a play he wrote, *Elverhøj,* in which the words of the character of Ebbesen to Agnete are literally Heiberg's asking Johanne for her hand in marriage. *Elverhøj* (The Elves' Hill) became Denmark's national play. Its fifth and final act reaches its peak in the most elegant and glittering of court dances which, to this day, are danced by the play's actors and by the stars of the Royal Danish Ballet.

Mme. Heiberg's remarkable career, fascinating as it is, does

Johanne Luise Heiberg, dancer turned actress.

not concern the dance follower except peripherally. She did become the undisputed star of the Danish stage. She was described as "the prima donna" of the Danish theater, and it was said that "she outshone everything and everybody." The foremost Scandinavian playwrights built their works around this remarkable performer of star quality, famed equally for her "splendor" as well as for the "dazzling," "gay," "witty," "charming" aspects of her art. When she retired as an actress, she became a director and was the first to stage Ibsen (although she did not like his plays) in Denmark. Her successor as the first lady of the Danish stage (and an incomparable Ibsen actress) was Betty Hennings, who had also started out her career, under August Bournonville, as a dancer and who had achieved ballerina status before attaining European fame as an actress.

On the other side of the scene, Bournonville found time to act as well as to dance and choreograph. In 1829 on his visit home before returning on a permanent basis in April of the following year, Johann Ludvig Heiberg gave August the role of Giovanni in his play *Princess Isabella*, in which August had two lines to say and a French romance to sing. Nine years later, when he was firmly established as the star and choreographer of the Royal Danish Ballet, he appeared in an entertainment in which he both acted and sang, and for this he was roundly booed by a claque of supporting actors and singers who felt he was invading their territories!

It is essential to note these interrelations of the arts in the Royal Theater, especially with respect to the Bournonville tradition and its path of evolution. Throughout his long career as choreographer and ballet director, Bournonville frequently used actors in his ballets and, conversely, trained his dancers to be actors. Not only had Mme. Heiberg been touched to tears by August's miming in *La Somnambule* on his return to Copenhagen, but she said in later years in her memoirs that she considered ballet training extremely important to actors and singers. She took pains to describe, in some detail, the kind of ballet instruction that would be advantageous to any career in the theater.

In matters of aesthetic tenet, Bournonville and the Heibergs shared a paramount one: Art is a question of the spirit, and the theatrical avenue to idealism is through realism. Mme. Heiberg was described as a realistic actress, yet the element of beauty was never absent from her interpretations. For the first and middle parts of the nineteenth century, Bournonville, Heiberg and the Danish theater itself bore the banner that proclaimed TRUTH AND BEAUTY. Mr. Heiberg and Bournonville had their differences starting in the 1850's when Heiberg assumed the directorship of the Royal Theater, but these were not of an aesthetic nature. Heiberg became incensed when Bournonville pushed for increasingly larger positions in the repertory and fought for the preeminence of ballet within the Royal Theater. He became sufficiently angry to remark to Bournonville that ballet was an inferior art. But the problem was simply that *both* men wanted to reign, although their kingdoms, drama and ballet, were actually *one* in theater.

This link between dance and drama underlies an understanding of and appreciation for the art of Bournonville. A century after his death, "Bournonville" means to most dancers outside of Denmark a "style," a special way of moving, of executing the steps of classical ballet. This viewpoint has originated because non-Danish ballet repertories present his work primarily in excerpt, in divertissements such as the popular pas de deux from *Flower Festival in Genzano,* a pas de trois from *La Ventana,* the tarantella from *Napoli* and other extracted dances. But these are only fragments of Bournonville. Even if they are delicious divertissements when taken out of context, they are not what Bournonville ballet is all about. The mimed antics of two street vendors in *Napoli* are as important to the ballet as the flashing tarantella, but if these hawkers are not played by consummate actor-dancers, the whole scene fails.

There are few, if any, ballet companies in the world capable of performing *total* Bournonville—the steps, yes, but not the acting passages and scenes—except for the Royal Danish Ballet itself. Bournonville's life and artistic achievements can never divorce completely the element of drama from pure dance. The ballerinas he guided to stardom were as skilled in the art of drama as they were adept in step, and the brilliant

Faust, a three-act ballet created by Bournonville in 1831.

male dancers who kept alive both the dignity and importance of men in the ballet during an era when the danseur, if he were permitted to function at all, was viewed with contempt as a necessary *porteur* for the goddess moving on a higher plane *sur les pointes,* under Bournonville represented virile heroes in both muscle and mien.

With Bournonville's assumption of his duties at the Royal Theater in 1830, his first ballerina was Andrea Kraetzmer, a gifted but difficult girl of nineteen. She had trained at the Court Theater ballet school with Johanne Luise Heiberg. When August danced in Copenhagen during the guest engagement in 1829, both women were thrilled by his dancing. Almost immediately, Andrea was enlisted as the first Bournonville ballerina. The new director-choreographer-premier danseur was twenty-four and recorded that Kraetzmer "illustrated my first performances on the Danish scene. She possessed a very rare mimic talent and she was a graceful dancer and interesting personality. Her performance of Virginie, Somnambule and [later] Marguerite in *Faust* belong to the best in this genre."

Before Andrea got to play Marguerite, she caused a minor upheaval at the Royal Theater and received for her efforts major punishment—she was sent to jail. The trouble started when Bournonville, while creating his three-act *Faust* in 1831, cast Johanne Luise as Marguerite and Andrea in a supporting role. The two young ladies never liked each other, and this projected casting was viewed by Andrea as an affront since she was the dancer and Johanne Luise was already relinquishing dancing for acting. But Bournonville was the boss—his maintenance of his authority increased rather than diminished with the years—and he ordered his dancer to rehearse as scheduled. She missed rehearsals and said she was ill. She was examined by the doctors at the Royal Theater who reported her to be in excellent health.

The Kraetzmer affair got so troublesome that it was brought to the attention of the king, who told her if she disobeyed she would be fired. She did indeed disobey and was committed to Blaataarn (the Blue Tower), a prison not only for murderers and their ilk but also for recalcitrant artists, for a two-month sentence. She enjoyed the dubious distinction of being referred to as "The Last Prisoner of Blaataarn," for the jail was not used again after her incarceration. She was, of course, fired. Her jail term completed, Andrea Kraetzmer was reinstated, became a notable interpreter of Marguerite and served the young Bournonville as his first dancer until one of the great ballerinas of the Romantic Age of Ballet emerged from the Court Theater school to make Kraetzmer and her colleagues fade away into history.

The newcomer was to become a dance immortal and to share with August Bournonville a special luster that would last for more than a century and a half. In its own time it was a tempestuous, tumultuous association that encompassed both love and lasting enmity, a blazing triumph and terrible exile. The lady in question was Bournonville's protégée, the star of his production of *La Sylphide*, performed to this day by major and minor companies around the world—*La Sylphide*, 1836, Lucile Grahn.

5

The Sylphide–
In Pursuit of a Dream

LUCILE GRAHN, born in Copenhagen in 1819, gave her first performance as a child dancer at the age of seven. In 1834 she made her formal debut at the Royal Theater. The next year she created her first major role, the part of Astrid in Bournonville's *Valdemar*, one of his most popular ballets and a work that represented a milestone in the Danish theater with respect to choreography, dramaturgy and staging. She was a pupil of Larcher during August's Paris years, but she became both a pupil and a protégée of Bournonville during the formative years—for each of them—from 1830 to 1837.

In his memoirs August wrote, "Lucile Grahn possessed all the qualities which are characteristic of a female dancer of the very first class. She was my pupil from her tenth year and she fulfilled all the promises to which her talent was entitled. It was really she who gave our audiences the first concept of female virtuosity in dance, and her noble performances of *La Sylphide* and Astrid in *Valdemar* make for an epoch in the annals of ballet."

Before Grahn, the Danish public had not seen ballerinas who were virtuosic dancers. Virtuosity was the province of the male dancer almost exclusively; the female was praised for delicacy, grace, lightness and, especially in Denmark, for mimetic or acting skills. Paris, of course, had already ushered in the age of the ballerina, and her newfound virtuosity on *pointe* a few seasons before with the sensational performance of Marie Taglioni in *La Sylphide* (1832) and the triumphant debut (1834), and meteoric rise, of Fanny Elssler. Their immediate forerunners had already experimented with dancing on toe, and the purely technical skill of the female dancer had captured the fancy of the public. Grahn displayed these new accomplishments for a delighted Copenhagen. In later years she was likened, not unfavorably, to the great Taglioni herself in matters of virtuosity, but European capitals, as well as Copenhagen, also praised her Danish dramatic skills. In London, at a later time, of Grahn's performance in the title role of *Eoline, ou La Dryade,* a ballet created for her by Jules Perrot, the press said she combined "the most graceful dancing with the most soul-despairing pantomime."

Such acting skill was essential to assuming the role of Astrid in *Valdemar,* for this particular role in a Bournonville work that would become a national favorite for the next fifty and more years would be the test of the Danish ballerina just as *Giselle* would test the dancing and acting merits of ballerinas outside Denmark for the next century and to the present. *Valdemar* was a splendid example of what was meant by the term "ballet" in the nineteenth century, for its component parts, of equal importance, were dancing, drama, music and design—and not necessarily in that order.

Valdemar, the first of many Bournonville ballets on Danish or Scandinavian themes, was drawn from Danish medieval history and was inspired by the novels of B. S. Ingeman. The music score was by August's contemporary, Johannes Frederik Frølich, who had just become a conductor at the Royal Theater following a few seasons of service as concert master (he was an expert violinist) and chorus master. He had composed the music for Bournonville's *Nina,* based partly on an older Galeotti ballet and partly on Louis-Jacques Milon's French version of the same story, which August knew from his Paris-London days. He also composed music for *The Tyrolians,* but *Valdemar* was his first major score, and it was an enormous success. He possessed a talent for dramatic music, and it was reported that he had the ability to "picture" situations in musical terms. Bournonville said of him, "At first he took the job of composing for ballet half in fun, but he soon realized

The immortal Lucile Grahn, Denmark's first internationally famous ballerina and the first interpreter of the Danish version (1836) of the milestone ballet, *La Sylphide,* which ushered in "The Romantic Age."

that he and I looked on situations in the same way. The audience was surprised and pleased and applauded *Valdemar* because of the music as well as for the ballet itself."

Many years later, August's daughter Charlotte noted that Frølich worked frequently in the Bournonville home in close collaboration with her father, but she recalled that "they often fought and screamed so much" that she feared disaster was imminent.

The designer of *Valdemar* also soared to fame. Troels Lund was made a member of the Royal Academy of Art on the basis of this ballet. The great Gothic hall in which three mighty kings meet was considered a remarkable achievement, as was the construction of the enormous chandelier that crashes to the stage as one of the kings, in the midst of a terrible battle, leaps upon a table and cuts the chain, resulting in the first instantaneous and complete blackout ever seen on the Danish stage. Since the theater in those days (this was pre-gas) still used Argand lights (oil lamps with chimneys and tubular wicks), a blackout was no small feat.

In matters of dramatic verity, Bournonville succeeded in staging a battle scene so effectively that he was asked to stage

Lucile Grahn in the title role of *Giselle*, the most popular ballet (choreographed by Coralli and Perrot) of "The Romantic Age of Ballet."

other such spectacles for pertinent scenes in Royal Theater productions. He noted that previously most staged battles evoked gusts of laughter from audiences and that his was the first such scene to have won their serious, even gripping, attention. Furthermore, he had one of the kings (Knud) killed right before the audience as the chandelier crashed. In casting the ballet for dramatic strength, he used two actors from the Royal Theater as two of the kings, and he himself played the third monarch. Grahn acted as well as danced the role of Astrid so successfully that it was instrumental in lifting her to a position of prominence in the Danish theater. Yet, in two years' time, her interpretation of this very role, significantly altered to suit herself, would cause the violent break between Bournonville and his favorite and would lead to her lasting exile from Denmark. But *La Sylphide* came first.

"I saw the Parisian *La Sylphide* only once," wrote Bournonville, "and my only good impression was Mme. Taglioni's extraordinary skill. And the fantastic scenery and machinery, both absolutely unobtainable for our own stage. Although I found the ballet very nice, I felt it would be better if I tried to do it in my own way. Besides, the score was too expensive [to obtain for Copenhagen], and James in the French version was only a pedestal for the 'prima donna'! The ballet's beautiful and poetical thought is that in pursuing an *imagined* happiness, he loses *true* happiness. This absolutely wonderful, poetical thought absolutely disappeared in the French version because we all looked at the virtuosity of the female dancers.

"At that point I had decided not to give *La Sylphide* on the Danish stage. What made me change my mind was the desire to present a very talented pupil, Lucile Grahn, who seemed made for the title role, whom I had modeled after the Taglioni ideal." Because of the expenses entailed in obtaining the original *La Sylphide* score (by Jean-Madeleine Schneitzhoeffer, a French composer and conductor) as Bournonville noted, it was suggested to him in Denmark that for his score he use a young musical talent, Herman Severin Løvenskjold, a twenty-year-old nobleman, who seemed suitable to the project.

"I made several changes in the plan," said Bournonville. "I gave the ballet a national color [Scottish] which is not to be

found in the Parisian version. I developed James' character, I thought out new dances and groupings and because the music was completely new, gestures and dances had also to be new. The staging too caused me the same amount of work and it all [developed] as if I had discovered the subject myself. I have been told that my ballet is not only different from Taglioni's [Filippo Taglioni, the choreographer of the 1832 Paris original] but as concerns the dramatic elements and the preciseness of performance, it wins the prize!"

Bournonville had taken Lucile to Paris earlier. He saw his single performance of *La Sylphide* and when, on November 28, 1836, he offered the premiere of his version at the Royal Theater in Copenhagen, he was accused of trying to imitate Filippo Taglioni! The Taglioni original had already been seen

42

Torch dance from Bournonville's *Valdemar,* a ballet on a Danish theme which became Denmark's national ballet in the last century and which introduced spectacular new stage effects.

in Berlin, London, New York, St. Petersburg and Vienna before Bournonville mounted his *La Sylphide,* but it was his production and choreography and concept that lasted. As the Romantic Age of Ballet faded away in Europe and in America in the face of realism in the theater, it was retained, preserved and cherished in Denmark, literally locked up in Denmark until modern times. In the 1970's attempts were made in France to restore the Taglioni original to the Schneitzhoeffer score, but the Bournonville *La Sylphide* by that time had become the definitive version for ballet companies staging it around the world.

Lucile Grahn, however, did not object to Paris ballet styles nor to the upward thrust, both literally with the increased use 'of *pointe* and in theatrical esteem, of the ballerina. She had triumphed in a Danish version of a Marie Taglioni role and she had been compared favorably with that queen of ballerinas. She felt herself too important for little Denmark and soon returned to Paris to study and to dance. She wanted to remain there, but she too was a subject of the Danish king and, perforce, was required to return for a royal gala. She brought with her to Copenhagen dances from Taglioni's and Elssler's repertories in order to display her dual mastery of the spiritual dance qualities of Taglioni, the "Christian dancer," and the earthy, fiery characteristics of Elssler, the "pagan dancer," as they had been described.

Bournonville and his rebellious student quarreled violently, but never more angrily than over her tampering with the role of Astrid in *Valdemar*. She tried to change the steps in order to display her newly accomplished Paris ballet skills. Their violent confrontation led each to write a furious letter to the direction of the Royal Theater. Bournonville's letter stated bluntly, "Astrid is no drunken bacchante nor a voluptuous *bayadère* but a graceful young woman. Is it not therefore exasperating to see a well-thought-out composition changed into a gymnastic, equilibristic exercise by attitudes which do not belong to me, with more walking on the *pointe* than I had prescribed and finally the intolerable squatting at each final movement!"

In 1837 she danced in Bournonville's *Don Quixote at Camacho's* (the last ballet that Bournonville staged from a Paris Opéra repertory), to music of Ludvig Zinck. This was her final association with the man who had trained her, guided her and created for her. The following year, she made her debut with the Opéra in Paris and signed a three-year contract with that company. Soon she was seen and applauded in theaters from London to St. Petersburg, with one of the highlights of her post-Danish career being her selection to appear in London in 1845 in the famous *Pas de Quatre* starring four of the world's five greatest ballerinas (only Elssler was missing) in a command performance for Queen Victoria. Here Grahn shared the stage with Marie Taglioni, Carlotta Grisi (the first Giselle) and the adored Fanny Cerrito. Grisi's husband, the brilliant dancer Jules Perrot, created the work and succeeded in placating all four temperamental ladies and presenting each in her finest style.

Grahn won plaudits for *Eoline* the same year and for another Perrot creation, *Catarina, ou la Fille du Bandit* (in which she danced while brandishing a musket), in 1847. She retired, of her own volition, in 1856. With her farewell, the Romantic Age of Ballet could be said to have come to an end . . . except in the Kingdom of Denmark.

The Bournonville-Grahn disputes did not terminate with her departure from Copenhagen to international fame. Even three years after her departure feeling ran high in theater circles in Copenhagen. She had treated Bournonville abominably but he, in turn, had been dictatorial with her. Each wanted to be the top figure in the Royal Ballet. Some of her most partisan followers never forgave Bournonville for taking a position that led to her leaving Denmark. One ardent Grahn admirer, Count von Schulenberg, headed a demonstration against Bournonville with near fatal results to the future of Danish ballet.

The count bought two boxes for a performance of *The Toreador,* Bournonville's newest and one of his most popular ballets, and gave all the tickets to a shoemaker with the proviso that he would gather for his guests people with the loudest voices available. Their job was to boo Bournonville on his entrance. The claque did its job: when Bournonville was borne in as the dashing toreador, a massive boo echoed through the Royal Theater. Bournonville was so furious that he removed his hat, walked to the Royal box and said, "What does Your Majesty wish me to do?" The king said, "Continue." But the next day, by his command, Bournonville was placed under temporary house arrest and subsequently handed his letter of dismissal from the king, who blamed his embarrassment about this involvement in a public scandal on Bournonville. The sentence finally resolved itself into a year's suspension without salary.

Bournonville could have remained in Denmark during his period of punishment, but he elected to go to Italy. His visit to Naples, where he fell in love with the city, the country and the Italians, turned out fortuitously, for it led to the creation of one of his masterpieces, perhaps his masterwork, *Napoli,* the

45

A later production of *Valdemar* with Maria Westberg, Bournonville's last ballerina discovery, as Astrid, the heroine.

three-act ballet that has remained a favorite of the Danish public and of Danish monarchs (the late King Frederik IX rarely missed a performance unless state affairs intervened), from its debut in 1842 through to the centenary of Bournonville's death in 1979.

As for Lucile Grahn, her revenge on Bournonville through a count, a shoemaker, a battery of booing voices and, of course, a king's anger did her little good. In the many, many years that lay ahead of her—she died in 1907 close to ninety years old—she always wished she could return to Denmark, but she did not dare. History has quite well proved that she was, or meant to be, a patriotic Dane, but somehow she became involved in

Over the decades, the role was a sort of yardstick by which new ballerinas were judged.

the independence movement of the duchies of Schleswig-Holstein, long under territorial dispute with Germany and subsequently ceded, after the war of 1848–1849, to Prussia. She never wore the German colors in a costume, as was reported, when dancing in Germany, but her reputation was tainted and she could not safely face her countrymen.

From shortly after the time of her retirement until 1861 she was in Leipzig. From 1869 to 1875 she served as ballet mistress at the Munich Court Opera, where she was associated with Richard Wagner in some of his opera stagings (she choreographed the Bacchanale in *Tannhaüser*). Bournonville traveled to Munich in 1869 to see a performance of *Lohengrin,*

47

Harald Scharff, one of the great male dancers of the Bournonville era, as Gennaro in one of the most popular Bournonville ballets, *Napoli.*

an opera he was scheduled to stage in Copenhagen. He was certain that he would see Grahn there. In preparation for their possible meeting, he wrote her a letter suggesting now that *thirty* years had passed since their breakup, they might once again be friends. At about the same time, she expressed the hope that "he'd burn in hell forever!" On his visit they did meet, and Bournonville's report consisted of the statement: "I reviewed our former acquaintanceship and our *best* memories in the most agreeable way."

Lucile Grahn, however, may have had the last word on the subject. During the season of 1896–1897 in Munich, an eighteen-year-old Danish dancer, Adeline Genée, soon to become the toast of London and New York, star of classical ballet and musical revues and vaudeville with equal success, walked into a shoeshop. She had already conquered the Munich public and critics who had not seen a dancer of her brilliance within living memory. In that shop she encountered one who lived only in history books and no longer in memory except for the few left who could recall the "golden age," Mme. Jung, the former Lucile Grahn. Young Adeline was captured by the power of her presence. It seemed apparent that she belonged to the theater, for although she was nearly ninety, she had dyed her hair and painted on a hairline to cover up its recession. The owner of the shoe emporium presented Adeline to the great old ballerina. While the younger Dane stood there in awe, Grahn complimented Adeline on her performance in Munich.

Grahn also talked about her past and how much she had

Sketch—J. L. Lund's design for the curtain of the Royal Theater, then and now.

gained by leaving Denmark to become an international figure with acquaintances, friends and colleagues of status and interest on the world scene. She referred briefly to her early years in Copenhagen, and then told Genée that she had felt forced to leave the Royal Theater, Copenhagen and Denmark itself because of Bournonville's "unwanted attentions." It is true that rumor had him in love with his pupil, and the gossip was that she had rejected his advances. But in the end it was not love but hatred and the plots, counterplots and scandals thus spawned that drove Grahn from Denmark forever and exiled Bournonville from his ballet, his theater and his homeland for a year. Perhaps like James in his *La Sylphide*, August Bournonville was in pursuit of an "imagined happiness" instead of that *truth* which, along with *beauty*, constituted the cornerstone of his art.

6

An Italian Ghost *vs.* Italy Alive

BOURNONVILLE, with his successful staging of *La Sylphide* and the triumph of his Danish national ballet, *Valdemar,* had put the past behind him. *Paul et Virginie, La Somnabule, Nina* and the like were ballets based on older French works he had seen and been involved with in Paris, ballets rooted in the pre-Romantic Age of Ballet. True, *Sylphide* was of French inspiration, but it was the cornerstone of a new ballet concept that Bournonville would carry to its fullest, most enduring expression.

Breaking with a French choreographic tradition—he held to the academic traditions of French classical ballet as represented by Vestris—was one thing. Breaking with Danish ballet tradition was another. His predecessor as ballet director and principal choreographer, Vincenzo Galeotti, was the first great director-choreographer of Danish ballet, and his reign, 1775–1816, was a long one. Yet once August Bournonville had assumed command, almost all of Galeotti's ballets, which numbered close to seventy (beginning with *The King's Hunt* in 1775 and closing with *Macbeth* in 1816), disappeared from the stage. The only one to survive to the present is *The Whims of Cupid and of the Ballet Master* from 1786.

Bournonville's ego as well as his ballet preferences had something to do with the disappearance of Galeotti, but there was more to it than that. Outside Copenhagen, and particularly in Paris, the ballet capital of the world, all of the old-time

51

classical ballets were swiftly disappearing, giving way to the new Romantic Age creations. Choreographers such as Filippo Taglioni—and there were several of them—made the change to the almost totally new choreographic and dramatic styles and to the introduction of the *pointe*. Galeotti was too old and his headquarters too distant to make change possible.

The young Bournonville, newly appointed to the Royal Ballet, "fought the ghost of Galeotti." Memories of the old man and of the old ballets constituted his only rival. "I fought the memories of the good old days," he said. "His works were praised more than they actually deserved. If I went through Galeotti's ballets scene by scene, group by group, I could not find anything really remarkable. However, I couldn't help admiring the enthusiasm and respect with which his name and his works were mentioned. I was often asked whether I was not going to stage some of his masterpieces and as I knew them quite well and my father and Mme. Schall would help me, I agreed to do the best of his ballets, and the one that suited my dancers was *Romeo and Juliet*.

"I treated the ballet with the utmost care. I did only little changes that even the master's admirers thought necessary. They had marvelous scenery and the performance itself was wonderful, but the ballet had lost its flavor. The story bored people and the details were no longer of interest, and the once much-appreciated songs with which the ballet was decorated were now looked on as ridiculous appendages. We gave four 'lukewarm' performances that were soon forgotten."

The Galeotti matter was not permitted to rest. August's daughter Charlotte, who became an opera singer, recalled a party given at their home at Fredensborg when a Professor Nielsen suggested reviving Galeotti. "My father," wrote Charlotte, "knew that the Galeotti ballets were old-fashioned and he did not believe he was capable of modernizing them. So my father asked Anna Nielsen, the actress, if she remembered Galeotti's most beloved ballet, *Romeo and Juliet*, and if she did, would she like to play some of the scenes with him right then. She had a very good memory, so they did several of the major tragic episodes completely accurate and with the traditional, inevitable little tripping steps just as in Casorti's pantomimes along with the invariable convention that every expression, every gesture be repeated three times! It was so comical that we all laughed and couldn't stop laughing. Professor Nielsen never ever again suggested that my father should stage Galeotti."

As late as 1866, on the fiftieth anniversary of Galeotti's death, there was a suggestion that "I should try to restage one of Galeotti's big ballets, and I must say that I was rather attracted to the idea," wrote Bournonville. It would have been a matter of redoing *Lagertha* sixty-five years after its triumphant premiere as the first ballet with a Nordic theme. "I went through the composition scene by scene and I realized—I cross my heart—that the best thing you could do for Galeotti and his renown would be to let his so highly praised works rest in peace beneath that laurel his admiring public had once planted to his glory.

"It is my absolute conviction that if I should try to make the present generation accept the Italian pattern in which these tragic ballets were constructed at the beginning of this century and if I revived—very accurately—the dances, divertissements and pantomimic scenes which made such an impression on our grandparents, my responsibility would be unbearable and the results would be boring. I realized [after these considerations] that I must refuse."

In a few years, with Bournonville's death, the fate of Bournonville ballets might well have echoed the fate of Galeotti's, for the Age of Naturalism had arrived and Bournonville's romantic-spiritual ballets appeared dated to many. But Bournonville was more fortunate than Galeotti, for he had no successor of stature. Thus Bournonville's ballets were not erased by a new and blazing talent but were retained, even in afterglow, as the best that Danish ballet could offer.

Bournonville's romanticism was indeed of a virtuous nature. In his first seasons as director of the Royal Danish Ballet he had remarked that he felt some of Galeotti's love scenes were too torrid and his heroines occasionally of questionable virtue. Hence when he staged his version of *Nina, ou la Folle par Amour* in 1834, he used as his model the 1813 ballet of Milon, which had become the rage of Europe, rather than the 1802

Augusta Nielsen in the popular folk-flavored solo, *La Lithuanienne*, a dance that is still performed.

Nina of Galeotti, because he felt that Galeotti's Nina was not at all times circumspect. He even had qualms about the theme of infidelity in *La Sylphide,* for although he introduced the realistic into his romantic ballets with remarkable and lasting success, purity was of deep concern to him.

His religious feelings ran deep, and he considered himself a good Lutheran. His stance, however, was more than a personal conviction—his concern throughout his career and his life was the status of his dancers as well as the stature of his art. He believed firmly what Antoine had told him of the dancer's profession: *"La carrière la plus glorieuse du monde."* He wanted others to believe it also. In the preceding century, artists of the theater were viewed as persons "of easy virtue," and something of that estimate carried over into the new century, especially in Paris and even as far away as Copenhagen.

August Bournonville, through his own religious principals, his public behavior, his ballets and his demands upon his dancers, strove for a new ballet era on the socioeconomic level.

He wanted ballet to be respected. He wanted dancers to be given the same treatment as that accorded a doctor or a minister. He did not want the male dancer to be looked upon as "half-man." And he fought ceaselessly for better financial conditions for all in the theater. In other lands, actors, singers and dancers were considered something less than first-class citizens. But thanks in great part to Bournonville, such attitudes did not prevail in Denmark. Mme. Heiberg, for example, actress and former ballerina, was regarded as a lady in her own right—the Bishop of Copenhagen attended her salon!

Bournonville's descriptions of his artists are indicative of his views as a solid citizen of Denmark. His ballets, unlike almost all of the ballets of the pre-Romantic Age with their gods and goddesses, kings and princes, dealt with ordinary people. His heroines might be mischievous or restless but they were virtuous and most assuredly virginal. And his heroes, even if they displayed human frailties, were manly and brave. Thus when he decried Grahn's tampering with the role of Astrid and described her abasing of the part to that of "a drunken bacchante" or a "voluptuous *bayadère*," he was expressing more than displeasure, it was revulsion. When he came to describe Grahn's major successor, Augusta Nielsen, he wrote many years later: "In her very short theater career, she left behind her a name synonymous with grace and lady-like elegance and lightness too. These characteristics made her an unforgettable Celeste in *Toreador*. She had many admirers, and young men paid court to her but she always refused them."

Bournonville stood solidly behind her in the one scandal that involved her and that brought her career to a much too early close. Prince Frederik Wilhelm of Hessen was in love with her and paid obvious court, but she rejected him completely. Yet the public seemed always eager for a scandal. In one ballet, Nielsen came on stage wearing a glittering diadem. The audience believed it to be an extravagant gift from the Prince of Hessen and, disturbed by such implications of immorality, chased her from the stage with screams of vilification. Bournonville wrote, "And so it was in February 1849, ballet lost its best dancer and the Prince lost his Augusta, and all that was left were the memories of a lovely woman, some discarded clothes and a diadem with false stones."

During her brief career, Nielsen won plaudits not only in Denmark but also in Sweden. In 1839 Bournonville traveled with a group of Danish dancers, including Nielsen and the ballerina virtuosa Caroline Fjeldsted, to Stockholm for a short engagement in a program that alternated with the opera *Robert of Normandy*. The opera was a smashing success because of a nineteen-year-old girl who stirred the audience to a wild ovation. Her name was Jenny Lind. But the Danish ballet artists had their own ovations, which they shared with a Swedish youth, Christian Johansson, a highly gifted dancer who had studied with Bournonville during an earlier visit to Stockholm in 1833 and who had returned with him to Copenhagen for a study period lasting until 1837. Johansson, only sixteen when he went to Denmark and twenty when he returned, had become a principal dancer with the Royal Swedish Opera Ballet and had advanced sufficiently to partner the great Marie Taglioni, herself half Swedish.

So it was that when Bournonville, Nielsen, Fjeldsted and the other Danish stars visited Stockholm in 1839, Johansson joined them not simply as a member of the host company but, more importantly, as one of Bournonville's most successful students. Two years later Johansson was invited to perform in Russia at the home of the Imperial Ballet in St. Petersburg, and such was his triumph that he remained there, a popular soloist. Of major pertinence to the Bournonville story is that in 1860 he began teaching at the Imperial School; in 1869, upon his retirement as a performer, he became a principal and most influential teacher there until his death in 1903. It was he who trained Mathilde Kschessinska (who became prima ballerina assoluta), Olga Preobrajenska (a great ballerina destined to become a major teacher herself) and a generation of dancers that included Pavlova, Fokine, Karsavina, Nijinsky and other international stars. Through him, Bournonville pedagogical concepts and training approaches spread far beyond Denmark to generations of dancers who, perhaps, never knew that the Danish king's ballet master was their ancestor.

In 1839 Bournonville was still in the good graces of his king, for in addition to conveying the superiority of Danish ballet to

Nielsen, "an unforgettable Celeste," as Bournonville
described her, in his *The Toreador*.

Sweden, he created for His Majesty and the Danish public his *Festival in Albano,* described as "perhaps his most beautiful work—breathing liberty and grace." Bournonville had never been to Italy, but this "idyllic ballet," as it was classified, had been inspired by the greatly beloved Danish author, Hans Christian Andersen, who had written about his extensive travels in Italy. The work was dedicated to another distinguished Dane, the sculptor Bertel Thorvaldsen. *Toreador* (Bournonville had never been to Spain either), a smashing success, was presented in 1840. And it was the following year, in a performance of his own *Toreador,* that his behavior in the presence of the king led to his suspension and an opportunity to see Italy firsthand.

"I have to thank the gods, and the little incident of the *Toreador,*" he wrote, "that I came to a country where the soul could find peace and function. I had read about this country but luckily not enough that I could not be surprised. If I were able to describe what I saw and what I experienced in these four months in the middle of the summer in Italy, I would rather first cancel the description and tell those who might want to go to the south the following: if you like the sun; if you like the seas; if you like the wonderful air, the flowers and these vivacious people, these picturesque groups, just go quickly to Italy and study nature."

Art as well as nature enthralled him as, like any tourist, he visited Roman, early Christian and medieval buildings, monuments and statues. For him they were very much alive, and he wrote, "You can hear all that is perfect speak from the walls, speak from the niches and speak from the pedestals." But most important were the people.

Humanity pulsed throughout all of Bournonville's ballets, for in the age of romanticism and fantasy he, unlike most of the other choreographers of the era, celebrated the human elements in his ballets. This was achieved not merely through the conflicts between the key characters, one real and one fanciful, but also through the supporting roles and, indeed, whole villages or communities. Even if the sites of his ballets were sometimes foreign—Italy, Spain, Belgium, Scotland, Russia—the communal expressions with their spirit, their warmth and their honoring of the human being were, curiously, very Danish, just as the separation between the Danes and their absolute monarch was minimal—they were on talking terms with him as they are with their constitutional monarchs today—and neighborliness was the order of things.

When in Italy, Bournonville found it perfectly natural to join the peasants in their street festivities while his fellow tourists, lacking that instant Danish friendliness, stood by. But as he shared the dancing with the Italian peasants, "the whole party applauded and cried, 'Viva! gracioso! bravissimo!' and that is really to have a success. My fellow passengers now realized who I was.

Caroline Fjeldsted, "ballerina virtuosa," as Birthe in *A Folk Tale.*

"During Pentecost and other processional days the peasants, pious and hilarious by turns, are always jubilant at the Monte Verde . . . like the Danish St. John the Baptist Eve [the night when bonfires are lit and all the witches in Denmark fly to their mountaintop in Germany] but multiplied a thousand times . . . and my third act [*Napoli*] is only a very faint picture of what you see on these summer evenings, and even the best theatrical effect is weak when compared with the color you will see in these places.

"The people are poor but they save their money for fiestas and they have bright costumes with many-colored ribbons. There are lots of carriages but in between are pilgrims with their cassocks and staffs and you will see different flags with saints' names and pictures printed on them. The pilgrims all wear a picture of the Madonna on their hats. In front and behind the pilgrims are rows of dancers who have promised the Holy Virgin a tarantella. And this tarantella is going to last from the mountains of Monte Verde to the beach of Santa Lucia!"

From Naples, his Napoli, Bournonville went to Capri, the scene of Act II of his forthcoming ballet. "In the Blue Grotto I dipped my handkerchief and my hands in the water and it seemed to me they came out blue. It is a solemn moment when you get up from your crouched position [as you come through the entrance] and the feeling that takes hold of you is a sort of . . . well, you forget everything that lies outside the grotto, either sorrow or joy."

Bournonville felt that history and nature were so intertwined in Italy, so rich in substance, that the romantic legends so important to Scandinavia were not required in a land that in itself was by nature romantic. "Here in Italy," he wrote, "the Madonna follows you everywhere—she is the confidante of loving couples, she protects the sailor. She reigns in all quarters.

"In my ballet, I wanted to describe Naples just as I saw it, Naples and nothing else. This little story of my *Napoli* was merely the ribbon in the braid but the knot was strong enough to hold interest and *it is very seldom you hit it just like that!* It became the favorite ballet of the Danes. Perhaps I could do

something far better but *never* something as *lucky* as this."
And Bournonville had every reason to be a trifle smug about
his success following his return from temporary exile due to
the displeasure of the king. While he was gone, the Royal
Ballet engaged Filippo Taglioni to stage the *Nathalie ou la
Laitière Suisse*, a ballet he had first done for Fanny Elssler in
Vienna in 1831 and the following year for his daughter, Marie,
in Paris. It was never a rousing success, for the French found
its virtues only in Marie's performance and a London critic
dismissed it as "insipid." The Danes liked it even less, for
Bournonville gleefully recalled, "My absence, Taglioni's *Laitière
Suisse*, the installation of the Italian opera and the finale of my
drunk-with-pleasure spirit of Act III of *Napoli,* gave *Napoli* a
fame that, perhaps, it might not have obtained elsewhere."

7

The Prices: Ballerinas, Danseurs, Actors

THE DECADE of the 1840's was of major significance not only to Denmark—a king died and absolutism with him—but also to August Bournonville as dancer, choreographer and family man. In 1830 he had married Helene Frederikke Haakansson, and the children began to arrive almost immediately. In 1843 he lost his beloved father, Antoine, at eighty-three. The entire family was very close, and Bournonville kept this part of his life private—not secluded by any means, but private. They entertained at Fredensborg and in Copenhagen, and numbered among their guests such celebrities as Jenny Lind and Hans Christian Andersen, along with collaborators such as Frølich and colleagues. But personal lives were kept personal until daughter Charlotte, years later, wrote her memoirs.

Theatrically, Bournonville capped his *Toreador* and *Napoli* triumphs with further successes ranging from popular divertissements to major ballets, some of them landmarks in the history of dance. His little *Polka Militaire*, a divertissement, had music by Hans Christian Lumbye, soon to become known as "The Strauss of the North." This popular and enduring dance—it survives to this day among popular Bournonville divertissements often presented in "highlight" programs featuring artists of the Royal Danish Ballet—was a favorite with Antoine and, on his deathbed, he asked his son to dance it for him. It seemed as if this dance symbolized for Antoine his own triumphant extension into the future, for his son had become a

Bournonville and his family (painting by Edward Lehman). Left to right, Vilhelmine (daughter), Mathilde (daughter), Edmond (son), August Bournonville, Therese (daughter); standing, Eva (sister of Mrs. Bournonville); sitting, Mrs. Bournonville (Helene), Mrs. Haakansson (Mrs. Bournonville's mother), Charlotte (daughter).

great dancer, even more famous than he, a far greater choreographer and, perhaps discernible to the old man, the greatest ballet master of the age.

As Antoine died, one hundred years of noble de Bournonville dedication to the art of ballet, beginning with Antoine's mother, the dancer-actress Jeanne Evrard, was marked. Curiously, almost mysteriously, but perhaps even more significantly, the *Polka Militaire* would mark yet another Bournonville ballet milestone three and a half decades later on the occasion of August's death.

The year following Antoine's passing, the sculptor Thorvaldsen died. He had brought fame and honor to Denmark and had been a special inspiration to August, who worshiped him. August had danced at his father's death, and he wished to honor a fellow artist by paying tribute in the way he knew best—through dancing. He stated that he wanted to compose

August Bournonville's daughter, Augusta. She hoped for a ballet career.

a dance that he would perform as Thorvaldsen's coffin was carried out of Our Lady's Church. The suggestion was deemed "unthinkable" and the offer refused. August could not understand why an artist who had given beautiful statues to people everywhere should not be accorded a beautiful dance as he departed from a world he had enhanced.

The year 1843 saw the premiere of *Erik Menveds Barndom* (The Childhood of Erik Menved), a four-act ballet based, as *Valdemar* had been, on one of Ingemann's historical novels. It was the third hit for Frølich (composer of *Valdemar* and *Festival in Albano*). But even with these successes, Frølich with his continuing melancholia, poor health and self-doubts could not face failure. Thus when *Rafael*, a three-act romantic ballet, failed miserably in 1845, one of Denmark's finest composers announced that he would never again create for ballet. Bournonville asked him if he would then turn to composing symphonettes, songs and the like, to which he replied with a firm "No." The exasperated August had good reason to snap, "Then what *will* you do?" The irritated composer shouted back, "Bite my nails!" When passions had cooled a bit, Frølich, who had served Bournonville as brilliantly as the choreographer had served him, declared that he loved Bournonville as a friend but hated him as a ballet master.

Choreographically, the decade closed, as it had begun, with a masterpiece by Bournonville. This one was not only destined to remain a lasting staple in the repertory of the Royal Danish Ballet but also to serve as a living chapter of ballet history that could not have been preserved through words or the then-existing methods of dance notation but only in remembered movement. The ballet was *Konservatoriet, eller et Avisfrieri* (The Dancing School, or A Proposal by Advertising). It was described in its early days as a vaudeville-ballet, and although it had a romantic tale to tell, the plot was centered in the second act. The first act of *Konservatoriet* is a reproduction, or re-creation, of a Vestris class exactly like that attended by young August Bournonville in Paris in the 1820's and remembered by him. Here, then, in *Konservatoriet* is the only surviving record of the classical French ballet school of the pre-Romantic Age of Ballet. This is history reported to us today in its own dance terms. *Konservatoriet* is usually presented now in its first act, although on special occasions Act II, with its charming behind-the-scenes romance, is given.

Konservatoriet, the last Bournonville ballet of the 1840's, also served to launch a new ballerina and, indeed, a whole family of ballerinas, danseurs and actors. This was the Price family from the public (horrors!) and not the Royal theater. Juliette Price became Bournonville's prima ballerina and his very special inspiration until an accident ended her career in 1865. Juliette was successor to the great Augusta Nielsen. Augusta had shared honors with Caroline Fjeldsted, whom Bournonville admired for both her virtuosity and her great talent as a mime—he recalled that in *Napoli* her "acting electrified her audience and her colleagues on stage." Juliette, although the undisputed star, shared the stage with her sister Sophie and her cousin Amalie and, on the male side, with her brother Valdemar.

Denmark's distinguished ballerina tradition had begun with Anna Margrethe Schall, the star of the pre-Romantic Age, who was a Galeotti ballerina. She had, of course, danced with

Antoine and, as a fascinating in-the-line-of-duty function, had auditioned Hans Christian Andersen, who, in his youth, had dreams of a career in dance. Fortunately for the art of literature, his dance days were of short duration. Schall, admired and beloved, was succeeded by the tempestuous and talented Andrea Kraetzmer, who briefly spanned the transitional period between two ballet eras, capably and sometimes violently, and

Antoine Bournonville's grave near Fredensborg.

then on to Grahn, the first great Romantic Age ballerina who was Denmark's own for a short and dazzling time before setting out to conquer the whole world of ballet.

But Bournonville, understandably, placed Juliette Price ahead of Grahn in his estimate of the great ballerinas of the era. He described her as "one of those priestesses of Terpsichore, after Marie Taglioni and Carlotta Grisi, who has come nearest to my ideal of a female dancer. Far from wanting to compare or measure her with these famous names who have their strength in quantity, I think I'm sufficiently impartial to judge her talent as well technically as aesthetically, and I must say that her dancing not only possesses the perfection of the 'school' but is also sparked by genuine feminine grace which has spread a poetical aura over the main roles in most of my compositions." Hans Christian Andersen described her as "the dancer with the gilded heart."

August had done as much for the male dancer. When he took charge of the company, as principal dancer as well as director, a critic wrote that "some of the old stiff legs got their élan back after August took over." When he retired in 1848, thirty-five years after his debut as a child dancer in support of his father (Galeotti's *Lagertha*), he had maintained in Denmark the high status of the male dancer while elsewhere, with the coming of the Romantic Age, the male became merely a support for the ballerina. The era of the eminence of the man in ballet, with its Vestrises (father and son), Duport, Gardel and others, came to an abrupt end. Only Jules Perrot (married to Grisi) and Arthur Saint-Léon (married to Fanny Cerrito), both splendid choreographers, survived the devastation caused by the female and her toe shoes. Only in the Kingdom of Denmark did the male dancer, still a hero, survive relatively unscathed.

August did not carry the banner of the male dancer by himself. Of course his ballets gave equal opportunity to the male, for although ballerinas may have been his inspirations, he himself was a dance star and he choreographed not only for himself but also for a distinguished chronology of Danish danseurs. Then too, he had his father as a model of a great dancer and a man who had described the dancer's life as "la carrière la plus glorieuse du monde." A contemporary of August's was Pierre Larcher, born in Hamburg but a pupil of Antoine in Copenhagen from 1811 onward. He became a solo dancer with the Royal Danish Ballet in 1823 and in the year that August returned to Copenhagen (1829) for his guest appearances prior to his appointment, he danced the role of Apollo in Bournonville's *Celebration of the Graces*. A few years later he was featured in *The Tyrolians*, Bournonville's one-act "idyllic" ballet to music of Rossini. Larcher, small and agile, was especially pleasing in demi-caractère dances. Bournonville himself admired him. "He had a modern swing to his dancing," August wrote, "strength and endurance which the public adored." Larcher was also Lucile Grahn's teacher while August was studying in Paris, and in one Scandinavian dictionary he and Barrez of Paris are listed as Grahn's teachers with no mention whatsoever of Bournonville! Presumably Grahn had supplied the editors with the information she wished included (and deleted).

Older than Larcher but younger than Antoine was Paul Funck—these three, of course, were the interim leaders of the Royal Ballet, between Galeotti and August. Funck was an interesting and, in a modest way, valuable link in the male generation of the Royal Ballet. He was a pupil of Antoine, a protégé of Galeotti, a dancer (described as "skillful but not very interesting"), a discoverer of talent (it was he who gave Johanne Heiberg the solo that released her gift for mimicry) and a choreographer of some distinction in the field of solo dances, incidental dances and divertissements. His *Zéphire et Flore*, a staging based on the enormously popular ballet by Didelot, was a great success in Copenhagen; his minuet and gavotte in the play *Elverjøj* (1829), surviving unaltered through the years, constitute in themselves an accurate record not only of the steps but also of the deportment, the bearing and the etiquette of court dances.

The male dancer of the longest duration and of major influence during the Bournonville era was Ludvig Gade, who was born in 1823 and died in 1897. Gade was by no means a premier danseur in the sense that both Antoine and August were great stage personalities, virtuosos and "heroes" in the repertory. Actually, Gade never reached the rank of solodancer —the top classification in the Royal Danish Ballet has always been solodancer, with those in the lower category described simply as balletdancers. Ludvig was one of August's first pupils and served the Royal Ballet from the time of his debut in 1836 to his retirement in 1890. His first major Bournonville part was in a pas de deux in 1844 in *Festival in Albano*. In the

Ludvig Gade as Bjørn in *The Valkyrie*. A great actor-dancer and unswerving devotee of Bournonville, he succeeded him as ballet director of the Royal Ballet.

years that followed, Bournonville found that his well-built, strong body and expressive face were perfect for mime roles such as King Svend in *Valdemar,* Bjørn in *Valkyrie* and the peasant Ole in *Brudefaerden i Hardanger* (Wedding in Hardanger) (1853). So accomplished was he in these and other dramatic parts that new generations of mimes studied his performances avidly.

Bournonville said of Gade, "He absolutely belongs as one of the most important forces in Danish ballet." When Bournonville went to Stockholm (1861–1864), Gade took over the directorship, and upon Bournonville's retirement in 1877 was appointed successor. Bournonville obviously approved the choice, for he said, "As a ballet director, he has maintained my works long after I left and I owe to his taste the fact that they still retain a certain amount of freshness and interest."

Many of the foremost male dancers under Bournonville were distinguished primarily by their acting skills. During August's own dancing days this was understandable, since leading roles were his. So he could be generous about male dancers excelling in other genres. One such dancer was Edvard Stramboe (the Elder), whom Bournonville found to have "an extraordinary dramatic instinct and expressive physiognomy, a talented mimic, perhaps the best that I ever met. His comic sense was bottomless and among a great many character creations, I must point out his masterly performance of the jovial Englishman in *Toreador*." Andreas Füssel was another first-rate mime admired by Bournonville because "he contributed to the importance of my ballets mostly as an actor. In dramatic situations he had strength, dignity and a highly developed plastic sense." Golfo, the villain in *Napoli,* was one of his most effective roles.

Once August had retired from the stage, new leading men had their opportunities in Bournonville ballet leads. Harald Scharf was one of these. He was very handsome, "full of life and imagination" as Bournonville saw it and, according to the master, "he is undoubtedly the best lover we have had since I left!" Scharf's career, starting in the 1840's, was splendidly successful, ending when he broke a kneecap in 1871.

It was in 1839 that Bournonville had heard and met Jenny Lind in Stockholm. The young prima donna and the Bournonville family became friends. She visited them in Denmark and, in 1843, Bournonville convinced her that she was ready to sing at the Royal Theater. He recognized that she possessed the unexplainable gift of electrifying an audience through the power of her voice. Charlotte Bournonville in her memoirs stated, "Of all memories from childhood, the greatest impression is of Jenny Lind singing, of her whole personality. To me she looked like someone from another world. And although

I was only ten when I first heard her sing, I not only remember all the songs but even the smallest shadings."

August had been urging Jenny Lind to make her Copenhagen debut at the Royal Theater, but she had seen Mme. Heiberg on that great stage and had been so impressed with her artistry that she was terrified to even think about performing in the same theater. Finally, in the fall of 1843, she was scheduled to appear. Nerves almost got the better of her; she began to weep, wring her hands, fume and fret. Bournonville offered to go to the theater and tell the directors that Miss Lind could not appear. But she rallied at last and said she would "give it a try."

The rehearsal went beautifully; the members of the orchestra applauded her. When she returned to the Bournonville home, she kissed August gratefully and said, "Don't be angry with me, my dear Mr. Bournonville!" In subsequent visits, she was always given the children's room at the Bournonville home since it was the biggest and best in the house. All of the children would trot into her room each morning before she got up to visit with her, to play with her jewels and to listen to her as she sang her morning hymns or rehearsed a role. Charlotte, who was going to become an opera singer, was "overwhelmed" with Jenny Lind and was allowed to attend all of her rehearsals and performances. She remembered that "when we left the theater after performances, the streets were absolutely black with people, and I remember these thousands of people crying when they simply saw Jenny Lind."

Single male admirers wept with uncontrolled passion when she sang or had palpitations of the heart when she passed by. One who was thoroughly stricken and smitten was a dear family friend, Hans Christian Andersen, and the Bournonville children would tease him unmercifully, and laugh behind his back, at his unrequited wooing. Charlotte wrote, "We liked him very much, my sister, brother and I, but of course we couldn't imagine him as a *primo amoroso!!* and we thought it would be fun to tease him. When Jenny Lind came to see us, he never stopped asking, 'Has Jenny Lind never talked about me? Has she never said, 'I like him'? But we said 'no' because although Jenny Lind did talk about him and liked him very much and

Harald Scharff, as Helge, in *The Valkyrie*, another immensely popular ballet celebrating Nordic roots.

admired his works, she was not in love with him."

The decade of the 1840's presided over more momentous events than Bournonville's choreographed triumphs, his rewarding collaborations, his associations with the great ones in the world of art, his happy marriage and family life, his immensely rewarding journeys abroad, his discovery and fostering of new talent. For the decade of the 1840's brought with it shattering events that changed forever the sociopolitical structure of Europe, that introduced a new order and that left no one, from king to commoner, unaffected. It affected Bournonville and the very future of the Royal Danish Ballet. The year 1848 was a time of revolution throughout most of Europe. France dismissed its "Citizen King" of eighteen years, Louis Philippe, its last monarch. In Austria, Franz Joseph, who was to rule for nearly seventy years, came perilously close to losing his throne the very year he ascended it. In still other lands, absolute monarchs faced restive subjects who had decided that the time had come for their kings to reign and for themselves to rule. Denmark did not go untouched.

Frederik VI had had a long reign (1808–1839). He was the monarch who had much to do with the destiny of the Bournonvilles in Denmark and August in particular, for it was he who made possible the invaluable ballet studies in Paris and it was he who recognized the fact that Denmark must have August Bournonville at home no matter how difficult, demanding and exasperating the young man might be. The reign of Christian VIII was short, less than a decade (1839–1848); unlike his father, who instituted some welcome democratic reforms in his kingdom, Christian resisted all efforts to have him relinquish certain of his absolute powers. Denmark was seething with unrest when he conveniently died. His successor, Frederik VII, was amenable to change—indeed, he seemed to welcome it—and in 1849 he cheerfully signed Denmark's constitution. No blood had been shed, no monarch deposed, no violent revolution generated. Absolutism was gone with the stroke of a pen, and the Kingdom of Denmark, with a dynasty dating back nearly one thousand years, continued comfortably as a constitutional monarchy.

The changes of 1849 did not leave Bournonville unaffected,

nor the Royal Ballet itself. In 1848 the Royal Theater was controlled, as it always had been, by the crown. In 1849 the Royal Theater came under parliamentary control, subject to the whims of politicians. Many members of parliament from the provinces saw the Royal Theater as an extravagance for city dwellers, an expendable luxury. In fact, one of the first acts of the new government was to cut the budget of the Royal Theater. And in the Folketing (the lower house of the then bicameral government), there was serious discussion about whether there should be a Royal Ballet at all. Bournonville was highly irritated by this attitude, for although his own social and humanitarian feelings ran deep and were in total accord with the new democratic structure of his country, he had no patience with an attitude that designated the arts as either an extravagance or a luxury. Like his father Antoine, he believed strongly in democratic processes, but both Bournonvilles—and Antoine was almost a revolutionary at heart—served and admired their monarchs. For them, kings and country were indissoluble. Besides, the new Frederik obviously had an eye for ballet because, after two unhappy royal marriages, he chose a dancer, Louise Rasmussen, to be his wife. She could not become queen, of course, so he made her a countess.

Democracy prevailed. Not only had king and commoner long been on friendly terms in Denmark, but Bournonville himself had never permitted a class system of any sort to affect his fostering of talent or his treatment of his dancers. With a disobedient Royal Theater star such as Kraetzmer, he could be severe in a moment of anger and see to it that she was imprisoned for disobedience, and he could take public park entertainers and elevate them, with the king's aid, to the highest positions in the Royal Theater. In 1848 he worked his own artistic revolution on behalf of democracy by espousing the talents of the Price family, especially Juliette and Valdemar, who had been trained as acrobats and pantomimists.

The Price family had arrived in Copenhagen in 1795, coming from London. James Price and his wife Hanne presented equestrian shows in the Deer Park. Another arrival in Denmark, this one from Italy, was Giuseppe Casorti, pantomimist and a celebrated Pierrot of the commedia dell'arte. The Casorti family introduced pantomime in the commedia dell'arte tradition to Copenhagen, where it exists to the present in the Pantomime Theater in Tivoli. They performed first at the Court Theater at Christiansborg Castle, then moved from there to a series of popular wooden theaters including the "Fun Theater" in the Vesterbro section of Copenhagen.

The Prices and Casortis joined forces for popular entertainments. James and Hanne Price—the Danes came to pronounce the name "Preesa"—had several children, among them James the younger and Adolph, the former becoming a famous Harlequin, the latter a great Pierrot. Young James sired Amalie while Adolph was the father of Juliette, Sophie and Valdemar. Most of the many children became professional performers as pantomimists, gymnasts, tightrope walkers and dancers, equilibrists, acrobats and, of course, dancers. They toured Europe constantly, traveling by sailing vessel and coach, and they could be found all the way from Scandinavia to Italy or to the forests and steppes of Russia (Amalie was born in St. Petersburg).

In Denmark the Prices enjoyed royal patronage, for Frederik VI attended performances in their wooden theaters and later, when the three Price girls were admitted as students to the Royal Theater, Christian VIII offered them his "royal protection." The move of some of the Prices in the direction of the Royal Theater was the result not only of new democratic tendencies and Bournonville's unbiased support of talent, but also of economic need. Fires in their wooden theaters were costly as well as dangerous, and the opening of Tivoli in 1843 as one of the greatest art and amusement centers in the world gave the Prices their most serious rival.

With opportunities deteriorating rapidly, the Price brothers asked Bournonville if he would take the three girls as his private pupils while they were still performing at the Casino in Copenhagen. After six months of intensive training, Bournonville asked the direction of the Royal Theater if his three Price charges could be considered for the roster of the Royal Ballet. The request was granted, and the three were accepted as students at student salary.

The famous Prices, Sophie, Amalie, Juliette,
in (appropriately) *Pas de Trois Cousines*.

So it was that in 1848 Frederik VII was crowned, Bournonville retired as a dancer and the Prices—or some of them—moved from their acrobatics and pantomimes in wooden theaters to the glitter of the Royal Theater itself. In 1849 Denmark received its constitution, the Royal Theater and its ballet passed from crown to parliament, the great Augusta Nielsen retired and Juliette Price, along with Sophie and Amalie, made their debuts in a new Bournonville masterwork, *Konservatoriet*. A momentous decade had ended. A new era for the Royal Ballet, for Bournonville and for the Prices was about to begin.

8

Around the World in Ballets by Bournonville

THE ROYAL BALLET survived the transference of authority from king to parliament because of pressures, especially by Bournonville, upon its membership. He had already brought the art of dancing to a plane of social acceptance—the women of the ballet were now regarded as solid citizens with none of the courtesan smears that tended to label them outside of Denmark. Despite his temperament, Bournonville too was a solid citizen, a respected family man, a good Christian and comfortably bourgeois. As the present-day dance critic Erik Aschengreen has pointed out, "The Bournonville ballets are built upon a Christian, idealistic foundation. Such a belief was characteristic of his time, as the clearly dualistic perception of life with its cleavage between body and soul was almost always connected with a religious or philosophical idealism." He then points to Bournonville's dramatic use of the Madonna image's powers to combat evil in *Napoli,* or how Hilda, the heroine of *A Folk Tale*, is drawn to Christian symbols.

Allan Fridericia, another of today's critics and researchers, notes that Bournonville ballets, in addition to their Christian symbols and strong moralistic principles, were concerned with ordinary people. The hero of *Napoli* is a poor fisherman; a mine worker is the key figure in *Kermesse in Bruges*; other ballets

79

The rarest Price of all,
Juliette, in a painting
by Hansen Balling.

focus upon farmers, vendors, sailors, millers, a bakery boy,
ordinary townsfolk.

None of these virtues, translated into balletic terms, was
completely lost on the members of parliament who now held
the fate of the Royal Theater and of the Royal Ballet in their
inexperienced hands. The king could urge but he could no
longer command. Bournonville succeeded in saving, building
and establishing his Royal Ballet, for it was truly his. Ebbe
Mørk, dance critic of *Politiken,* author and lecturer, brought
to my attention a revealing comment by one of his journalistic
forebears, Colin. In writing an obituary in his column of
December 1879 in the publication *Here and There,* Colin said,
"He [Bournonville] conquered everyone except parliament." He
then went on to say that Bournonville's genius as artist triumphed over the reluctance of parliament, and his unflagging

determination not to permit the government to strangulate the ballet resulted in the accomplishment of his dream: to create a Danish national ballet on the level of opera and drama. He did more than that: He made the Royal Danish Ballet the major component of the Royal Theater itself.

The king's ballet master was inarguably democratic. He not only fought for the prestige of the Royal Ballet, but he battled with equal and perhaps even greater fervor for his dancers' working conditions. Under his regime salaries were raised and fringe benefits bettered, and no one was barred from the

Juliette Price as Ragnild, the heroine of the Norwegian-inspired ballet, *Wedding in Hardanger*.

The famous Mirror Dance from *La Ventana*, with Sophie and Juliette Price.

Juliette Price, "a creature of spirit as well as of body," in *La Sylphide*.

Royal Ballet because of class distinctions. He was criticized for taking the Prices from "meaner" conditions and environs into the Royal Theater, but his faith in his own eye for talent and his deep democratic instincts paid off. Later he said of Juliette Price, "She helped me fight the animosity of the adversaries of the ballet, for she has helped to show that dance is not merely a frivolous lust for the eye." Even before members of the Price family joined the Royal Theater, Bournonville had said that their "pantomime theater is art," and had capped his comment with an almost sacred name from the past: "The language of pantomime is the language of Galeotti."

The Prices soon became the performing backbone of the Royal Ballet. Valdemar, in due course, became as important as the three Price girls. He had begun, with the family in the Fun Theater, as Cupid in *Pygmalion*, as the child (a part he loathed) in *The Brazilian Ape*, as an equilibrist, a dancer in the Price ballets and in a variety of roles in the Casorti-modeled harlequinades and pantomimes that the Casortis and Prices had long offered in their various pantomime theaters. When Bournonville created *Kermessen i Brugge, eller De Tre Gaver* (The Kermesse in Bruges, or The Three Gifts) in 1851, there were two Prices in the cast: Juliette, the star, and Amalie. The next year (1852) four Prices—Juliette, Amalie, Sophie, Valdemar—were listed for the premiere of *Zulma, eller Krystalpaladset* (Zulma, or The Crystal Palace in London), inspired by the great Exposition of 1851 in London where the Crystal Palace was thought of as the eighth wonder of the world. There were Prices in *Wedding in Hardanger* (1853) in which Juliette played the leading role of the Norwegian Rahnild; *Et Folkesagn* (A Folk Tale) (1854), a Danish ballet with Juliette as Hilda; the Oriental *Abdallah* (1855) with Juliette as Irma and sixteen-year-old Carl Price as a Negro slave. Julius Price, a cousin of Juliette, was also one of the Royal Dancers, giving the Prices, along with another sister of Juliette, Mathilde, a roster of seven within the Royal Ballet.

Kermesse in Bruges, a three-act romantic ballet that has survived to the present day, was created for Juliette Price. She had made an instant success in *Konservatoriet*, but with *Kermesse* it was inarguable that she was not only a worthy successor to Augusta Nielsen but a very special artist in her own right. The ballet, set in Flanders of the 1600's and centered upon a fair associated with a saint's day, told the story of an alchemist who granted three gifts to three worthy brothers. One brother received a ring that made all the girls fall in love with him; the second received a sword that made him invincible in combat; the third accepted a fiddle that caused anyone who heard it to dance. The alchemist's daughter is the heroine. For the final scene, familiar figures from the great paintings of Flemish masters join with everyone else in dancing to the irresistible fiddle.

Bournonville, who had visited Norway briefly in 1840, returned in 1852 for a tour, featuring four Prices and Edvard Stramboe. Norway, which had belonged to Denmark before being ceded to Sweden in 1814, loved the Danish choreog-

rapher and he, in turn, thought of Norwegians as cousins. He brought with him on this tour ballet stagings of Norwegian dances, and while there discovered for himself the work of Adolf Tidemand, a gifted painter whose "Brudefaerden i Hardanger" painting gave him the title and suggested the story for his next ballet. Both the painting and the tale reflect a kinship with a much earlier romantic comedy, *La Fille Mal Gardée* (a 1786 ballet that Bournonville must surely have seen somewhere in Paris or on his travels elsewhere), both about a girl who loves an impoverished farm boy although betrothed, against her will, to an undesirable man of wealth. The finale for Bournonville's ballet included not only a happy ending for the young lovers but also a divertissement of Norwegian dances, which contributed to a work that proved to be a lasting favorite with the Danish public.

A Folk Tale, created the following year, was Danish to the core. Set in Denmark of the 1500's, it is a fantasy about a noble's child who is switched with a troll. The child is reared as a fairy and the troll as an heiress, with all being sorted out at the close. Juliette, spiritual, light and fragile, danced the role of Hilda, who believed she was a fairy creature. Petrine Fjeldstrup, a popular dancer in the company, played the troll who was genuinely convinced she was a noblewoman.

The summer of 1854 Bournonville paid a visit to Vienna. He disliked the ballet he saw, but he was offered such a handsome contract that he agreed to work there for a year and to stage three ballets from July 1855 to July 1856. The experience was not a happy one, for the Viennese found Juliette much too mild for a taste geared more toward the fiery Fanny Elssler; they tolerated *Toreador* and they hated *Abdullah*. Only *Napoli* was a success, *Napoli* and one of the Prices, for the Viennese public went wild over Juliette's young cousin, Julius. Vienna had seen no male dancer of his presence and accomplishments—although Copenhagen viewed him as merely competent —and asked him to stay. Julius remained in Vienna for the rest of his life. The other Danish dancers were delighted to return home.

The greatest of the male Prices, Valdemar Price, the handsome, virile star of *Napoli.* "At thirty-two he at last became a star."

Bournonville's travels, his voracious reading, his knowledge of painting and sculpture, his broad musical background enabled him to bring the world to Denmark through his ballets. These were not superficial excursions, for August was always profoundly concerned with the customs, the characteristics, the feelings of a people. Today it might be said that he was not content with exotic surfaces but, as far as the ballet idiom of the day permitted, was concerned with reasonably accurate ethnic reporting. This was certainly true of Italian researches and the resulting *Napoli,* and it would be true of his very last ballet, *From Siberia to Moscow* (1876), reflecting the keen observation, the mastery of detail in gesture and setting of an old man still possessed of the fervor of a youthful explorer.

Italy was explored not only in *Napoli* but also in the earlier *Festival in Albano* (rooted only in readings), and in the tremendously popular *Flower Festival in Genzano* (1858), which has given the world of ballet one of the most popular divertissements of all time, the pas de deux. Elsewhere he celebrated Norway not only in *Wedding in Hardanger* but also in *Fjeldstuen, eller Tyve Aar* (The Peasant Hut, or Twenty Years) (1859); Austrian and gypsy dancing in *I Karpatherne* (The Carpathians) (1857); Oriental themes in *Abdullah* and the first two acts of *Zulma;* Paris in *Konservatoriet;* Spain in *Toreador* and *La Ventana* (1854); and Greece, England, Scotland, Germany and more in other ballets. In *Fjernt Fra Denmark, eller et Costumebal Ombord* (Far from Denmark, or A Costume Ball on Board) (1860), for example, there were dances that included the Negro, American Indian, Hindu, Spaniard and Eskimo! To project this Cook's tour in ballet, Bournonville assembled four Prices—Juliette as Rosita the heroine, Sophie, Carl and Valdemar—plus a corps of genuine cadets from His Majesty's Naval Academy. It was reported that the cadets loved their unique experience with choreographic discipline.

Wherever his travels, real or imagined, took him, Bournonville was very much the family man, and there was no place he loved more than his home at Fredensborg, first in the wing of the castle and then in the large white house in the adjacent village. Although he wrote little about his own family, his

Far From Denmark (1860), a sketch of Act I, with the
Danish ship in the harbor.

More than a century later, Act I of *Far From Denmark,* with
Vivi Flindt as the reclining ballerina.

Act II of *Far From Denmark* and the
scene which delivers the promise of the
ballet's subtitle, "A Costume Ball on Board."

daughter Charlotte reports about their way of life as well as
their glamorous guests. She tells how grandfather Antoine
was both loved and respected by his children and his grandchildren, and that his one quirk was that the word "old" never
be used in his presence. Properly obedient, his fun-loving
grandchildren, in reassessing the traditional name of Denmark's first king, Gorm the Old (circa 950), addressed Antoine
as "Gorm the Young."

Making a home for Antoine, August, a growing family of

children, assorted relatives and guests was August's wife, Helene Frederikke (or Helen Frederika) Haakansson, whom he had met in 1829 during his guest appearance with the Royal Danish Ballet in Copenhagen and whom he married upon his return as ballet director of the company in 1830. Helene had been born in Skaane, Sweden, in 1809, of an un-married woman and an unknown (or unnamed) father. Augusta was the Bournonvilles' oldest daughter, Charlotte their second. According to Charlotte, her mother was a warm-hearted housewife, much more easygoing and casual than her very precise and punctual husband. It was not uncommon for August to pace back and forth or to restlessly read a book while waiting for his wife to finish her preparations for attending social events. The two were deeply fond of each other, despite rumors that Bournonville's attention was occasionally attracted by other ladies. Charlotte tells of an occasion when her father lost his wedding ring while swimming. He was despondent over the loss, but Mrs. Bournonville bought him a new one and told him that she was delighted to become engaged to him all over again! Helene, a real beauty as a girl, aged with grace—she died in 1895 at seventy-six—and if there were hints that her husband had romantic leanings toward Lucile Grahn and other fascinating women, it never bothered her for long. She often traveled with him, she accompanied him to church until his dying day, and unsung though Helene Frederikke may be, she was as devoted to August Bournonville as he was to his lifelong mistress, the Muse of Dancing.

August, the father, was as deeply involved with the lives of his children as Antoine had been a guiding force in young August's life. Charlotte was to become a singer, and August could be helpful there because he too had almost become an opera star instead of a dancer. But his daughter Augusta seemed bent on a career in dance. At fifteen, August permitted her to go to Paris for ballet studies, but he placed her in the care of her Aunt Eva and provided her with an elaborate series of instructions contained in a booklet he titled "Souvenir de Ton Père." This was in 1846, slightly more than a quarter of a century after his own first visit to Paris in the protective company of his father. His booklet gave her guidelines on study, etiquette, ladylike behavior and the nature of art, and insisted upon her observance of daily prayers and church (Lutheran) attendance.

But there was to be no Bournonville who would ever achieve the stature or the fame of August, although the family could boast of producing men and women who contributed commendably to arts, science, business and family life. One, however, achieved a certain notoriety. A granddaughter, Eva, was arrested in London during World War I as a German spy. When she heard her death sentence handed down at Old Bailey, she fainted; when brought to, she asked for her furs! The sentence was not carried out, and it is said that she is living, at past one hundred years, in Stockholm.

Bournonville's theatrical family was, of course, as important to him as his own private family comfortably housed at Fredensborg. So when injury or disaster or inevitable change touched their ranks, he was forced to regroup and refocus his attention, his concern, his discipline, his expert training and the paternal love of a ballet master on his theater children, and he thought of them as just that. Kraetzmer, Heiberg, Grahn, Nielsen had all gone, but with all the talented Prices now associated with the Royal Ballet and Juliette as his ballerina, his inspiration, his favorite theater child, it seemed as if his worries were ended for the foreseeable future. It was not to be so.

In 1865 Juliette Price, while dancing one of her greatest roles in the ballet created for her, *Kermesse in Bruges,* fell. The ethereal ballerina, light-footed, aerial as gossamer, a creature of spirit as well as of body, slipped on a petal fallen from a flower. The resultant ankle sprain never healed. One year later, Juliette Price at thirty-five retired from the stage. She had been Bournonville's ballerina for only six years, and in that short span the king's ballet master had made her a star and, perhaps unsuspected at the time, a lasting legend in the history of romantic ballet.

Bournonville could not afford to mourn the loss of his favored dancer. As ballet master he had to find more than a passing substitute. An understudy would not do. He needed someone who was, or could become, a ballerina, an interpreter

The second Bournonville home—this one in the village outside the castle grounds—big enough to accommodate August's ever-growing family and social responsibilities.

of his ballets, masterpieces of the past and masterworks yet to come. A revival of the great ballet *Valdemar* was scheduled, and Bournonville wrote, "The biggest problem was to find an Astrid since Juliette Price was retiring with an injured foot." None of the solo dancers or supporting leads in the company was capable of doing the role of Astrid the way he wanted it done. "I had a happy inspiration," he wrote. "I looked at a very young dancer and found that she was a possessor of a certain rhythmical swing and that in her blonde appearance there was present that inexplicable something that was apparent so early in Jenny Lind!"

The very young dancer was Betty Schnell. She made her debut in *Valdemar* at sixteen and, despite her seeming immaturity, she communicated through "a language that found its way to all hearts." The only flaw was that two muses had equal claim on her, and long before he wished to do so, Bournonville had to relinquish her to the muse who invited her to speak in a different language. As Betty Hennings, she became the greatest interpreter of Ibsen and one of the great actresses of the century . . . and Bournonville had to look about him once again.

9

The Beautiful,
the Graceful

BETTY SCHNELL (later Hennings) was born into a poor family. Her grandmother was a cleaning woman (often assisted by Betty's mother) at the Royal Theater and her father, who had started out as a tailor, later ran a restaurant and spent his last years as an usher at the Royal Theater. Like her ballerina-actress predecessor, Johanne Louise (Pätges) Heiberg, she passed her childhood summers in Copenhagen's Deer Park at a tent refreshment stand run by her parents. And, like Johanne before her, she succeeded in enrolling in the Royal Ballet School where her talents attracted the attention of both Bournonville and Professor F. L. Høedt, who preceded Johann Ludvig Heiberg as theater director.

Betty was seven-and-a-half when she entered the school. At nine she made her debut in the Holberg comedy *Masquerade*. This was in 1859, and Høedt, convinced of her great potential as an actress, both encouraged and coached her, coaxing her into the orbit of drama. Meanwhile, Bournonville saw in her the makings of a prima ballerina. Always more concerned with spiritual, ethereal qualities in his female dancers, and also demanding acting skills of them, he was not at all put off by a ballet technique that was not and never would be that of a virtuosa such as Grahn or Fjeldsted. So when fate removed Juliette Price from the stage and a new Astrid was needed, Bournonville was able to sway Betty, and "her rhythmical swing," as he described it, away from drama into ballet.

Betty was barely sixteen when she assumed the lead in *Valdemar*, once regarded as Denmark's national ballet but now forgotten. Bournonville had to silence those who doubted the wisdom of his casting with his words: "It is the spirit rather than the body which gives scenic art its life and charm." The late Robert Neiiendam, theater historian and distinguished archivist, wrote of her: "She may not have possessed choreographic mastery, but she did combine a peculiar mixture of purity and grace with the power of expressing faith and enthusiasm . . . there was poetry in her slender form, leaving an impression in the observer's mind of virgin purity; her glance had the same expression as the French sculptor Paul Dubois has given to his Jeanne d'Arc. . . . Young poets and writers fell in love with her eyes, where both innocence and determination shone."

Bournonville was affected by these eyes with "an almost unearthly expression," a mystique she shared, in the ballet master's opinion, only with Jenny Lind. Soon after her triumphant debut as Astrid, Bournonville wondered "how far the genius of this scene shall carry Betty Schnell." Interest was enormous, for none of her predecessors, it was said, had ever made such a deep and refreshing impression in the role. "I hope," said Bournonville, "that this young artist will keep the promises revealed at her debut. I don't know which way her talent will develop—the mighty muses of drama and dance both want to possess her—but whatever way, she will be a gem on the Danish stage."

Betty danced for a few seasons, excelling in *A Folk Tale*, *Far from Denmark* (in which she played a cadet!) and the new (1868) ballet on a Nordic theme, *Thrymskviden* (The Ordeal of Thrym). It was not simply the lure of the other muse that got Betty away from dance and into drama. Health was a deciding factor. Her lungs were weak, and the very last ballet that Bournonville created for her provided very easy dancing and extended mime scenes. "I was aware," said Bournonville, "how during this past season her breathing became difficult, and I thought that if she continued to dance she might be in considerable danger. How lucky she has been trained for drama! She has left ballet but she has retained her

Betty Schnell, extraordinary ballerina, metamorphosed into Betty Hennings, the greatest actress of Northern Europe and the supreme interpreter of Ibsen. Here she dances the defiant tarantella in Ibsen's *The Doll's House*.

lovely gifts, and I'm happy to say her debut in drama was very successful."

Betty Hennings, the actress, became the most celebrated interpreter of heroines in the plays of Henrik Ibsen during the 1870's, 1880's, 1890's and even into this century. She made her Ibsen debut as Selma in *The League of Youth* (1876), one of his earliest figures of the emancipated woman. In 1879 she achieved unequaled success in Northern Europe as the fully emancipated Nora in *A Doll's House*, in which, of course, she danced the famous tarantella. Her final Ibsen part was Mrs. Alving (1903) in *Ghosts*. Celebrated throughout Scandinavia, she enjoyed successes in other lands; although she spoke only Danish, Berlin and Prague "were impressed," in the words of Robert Neiiendam, "by the beautiful human character behind her art, and by the speaking expression of her eyes. The conquest was the greater in that she could not capture these foreign audiences by passionate violence but must content herself with winning their admiration by her nervous acting, her intelligence, her imagination and her electrifying energy."

That Betty Hennings was an actress while still a dancer is attested to by a story that she, as a very old lady, told to Mrs. Karen Neiiendam. At a performance of *Valdemar*, something had gone amiss with Astrid's costume and, between scenes,

The young Hans Beck in Bournonville's *The King's Volunteer Guards on Amager*. His debut in 1879 was the last performance Bournonville attended.

Betty rushed to the costume room to have it repaired. On her racing return she forgot a prop, a silver cup she needed for the next scene. Undaunted, she resorted to mime to establish the presence of the cup. She felt she had been successful until she met Bournonville at the stage door at the close of the performance. "He had seen what I had done," she told Mrs. Neiiendam, "and he boxed my ears!" But Mrs. Neiiendam also witnessed the dancer in the actress, for when she and other guests visited the eighty-year-old Betty Hennings, "she greeted us by curtseying all the way to the floor and then getting up again!"

There were always Prices available to Bournonville. He had lost Juliette—his last major work for her had been *Valkyrie*—but in the same ballet he had given her brother, Valdemar, his first starring role. He had been a slow developer. At thirteen he was an aspirant with the Royal Ballet; at twenty he was promoted to balletdancer. From then on he danced sometimes in the back row of the corps de ballet, occasionally in small parts, and was valuable as a replacement. In *Valkyrie,* Bournonville starred his sister and gave him his first important new role. He was an instant, if delayed, success. He followed this with an equally successful appearance with his sister in *A Folk Tale*. In the 1866 revival of *Valdemar,* in which the teenage Betty Schnell made her unforgettable debut, Valdemar Price came into his own with his interpretation of the role of King Valdemar. Thus at thirty-two he at last became a star, a romantic hero. He was not a virtuosic dancer at all, and neither was Schnell, but he was a fine dancing actor and an impressive stage personality. The role of Thor in *Thrymskviden* added to both his stature and his popularity, and he was very much the hero of the 1871 ballet—Bournonville was then sixty-five— *The King's Volunteer Guards on Amager,* another truly Danish ballet that has retained its popularity for more than one hundred years. Valdemar was cast as the dashing officer, modeled after Edouard Dupuy, Antoine Bournonville's old comrade-in-arms in the battle of Copenhagen in 1801.

It was in 1871 that Bournonville also lost his great male dancer, Harald Scharf, due to a broken knee. Scharf, who had begun his career in the 1840's, had succeeded Bournonville as principal male dancer of the Royal Ballet. It took two dancers to succeed the perennially popular Scharf, a virtuoso as well as a superb actor. Valdemar Price fell heir to most of Scharf's character parts, and Daniel Krum, at twenty, assumed Scharf's virtuoso assignments. Bournonville described Krum as "one of my thoroughbred dancers." He entered the ballet school at seven and immediately caught the eye of the old ballet master, who trained him carefully and gave him the engaging part of the Dancing Master in *Konservatoriet* for his debut. He advanced swiftly to the rank of solo dancer and excelled in such ballets as *Valkyrie* and *Flower Festival in Genzano,* a work that provided a perfect showcase for his slender, handsome presence and his high technical skill. He was an inferior mime (Valdemar, a superior mime, was never made a solo dancer, although he was regarded as the male star of the company). Something of a protégé of Bournonville, Krum tried his hand at choreography at the master's insistence. But he proved to be no better at choreography than at acting. His forte was dancing and, later, teaching at the Royal Ballet School. He committed suicide in 1887 and was succeeded as first dancer by one of the most important beings in the history of the "Bournonville School," Hans Beck.

Valdemar Price danced with Betty Schnell (Hennings) in Bournonville's 1870 ballet *Cort Adler i Vendig* (Cort Adler in Venice), a three-act ballet about a Norwegian naval officer which closed with the tableau of a sea battle between Turkish and Venetian ships. However, spectacular staging could not carry an otherwise poor ballet. Valdemar Price achieved success the following year in *The King's Volunteer Guards on Amager*. And that same year, 1870, Betty Schnell made her debut as an actress and went on to great fame in drama and to a long, happy life that came to an end as she approached ninety.

With Betty Schnell gone, Bournonville had to find a new ballerina, his last. He found her in Sweden.

Sweden was, of course, close to Bournonville. His father had had his first major successes in Stockholm, his own mother was Swedish, he had taken Danish dancers to Sweden for performances on several occasions and had brought Swedes back to Copenhagen—Christian Johansson among them—for

Maria Westberg, star of Bournonville's last ballet, *From Siberia to Moscow*.

further training in the Bournonville School. His wife too was a Swede. From 1861 to 1864 he had been in Sweden under contract, for his Danish contract with the Royal Theater in Copenhagen expired in 1861. He had thought that his career as ballet director-ballet master of the Royal Danish Ballet would end at that point, and so he had planned for his last ballet to be Nordic, elaborate and full length (four acts). It almost did not get on stage because of a budget crisis during an economy-oriented period. At the last minute King Christian VII brought royal pressure to bear on the director of the Royal Theater, and the great dramatic ballet that was to star Juliette and Valdemar Price and was to celebrate great Norse legend finally materialized in the fall of 1861. Following its smashing success, Bournonville left immediately for Sweden.

While he was in Sweden, Bournonville's beautifully trained company, his several brilliant Prices (Juliette and Valdemar leading them) and Ludvig Gade as director of the ballet saw to it that a repertory of a dozen Bournonville works was expertly performed. Bournonville himself mentions how beautifully Gade cared for his creations during this period and after his retirement. To replace Bournonville creatively was impossible, but Gustave Carey, a French dancer who had at one time studied with Bournonville, came to Copenhagen as choreographer and stager. He gave the Royal Ballet its first *Giselle* at the Royal Theater (it had been presented earlier at the popular Casino where the Prices had once danced and where Bournonville had made the initial version of his mirror dance for *La Ventana*). *Giselle* was not to the liking of Copenhagen ballet followers who, seeing it again twenty years after its sensational Paris premiere, possibly found it too dated, too representative of an age that was slipping away.

Carey, during Bournonville's absence, also produced original ballets and adaptations of ballets popular in Paris. Although his own virtuosity as a dancer and the virtuosic demands of his choreography at first titillated the taste of the Danish public, it was not to be a lasting appetite. Bournonville was missed. Carey was dismissed, or at least his contract was not renewed, and Juliette, together with Gade, kept ballet going à la Bournonville until the master's contract was up in Stockholm and he was able to return to Copenhagen. He had no Danish contract and presumably he was retired as far as the directors of the Royal Theater were concerned. But while he spent more than a year at Fredensborg doing extensive writing —he authored volumes on his theater life (*Mit Theaterliv*, written 1848, 1865, 1877), on his choreographic studies and principles, and wrote on other matters—his influence at the Royal Theater was obvious. The foolishness soon came to an end: The Royal Theater needed him and he needed the Royal Theater. A new contract was signed.

No sooner had Bournonville resigned as director of the Royal Ballet and resumed his duties as principal choreographer than his beloved Juliette had her fateful injury. Barely four years after that, his newest discovery, Betty Schnell, was also gone. He could not, at the moment, find the replacement he needed at home. He turned to Sweden and invited a sixteen-year-old dancer from Stockholm—Betty Schnell had been just sixteen when Bournonville elevated her to stardom—to come to Copenhagen for intensive studies and coaching. Maria

Westberg accepted the offer. She had been trained at the Royal Opera in Stockholm under the guidance of a teacher who had once been a Bournonville pupil, the ballet master Sigurd Lund.

In 1871 Maria made an enthusiastically applauded debut in *La Sylphide*. Later the same year she scored again in Bournonville's new three-act ballet, *Et Eventyr i Billeder* (A Fairytale in Pictures). She was tall, slender, very Nordic in appearance and a splendid technician. Her mime skills were less developed; although she effectively played Astrid, Hilda and Celeste (the heroines of *Valdemar, A Folk Tale* and *Toreador*, respectively), she had insufficient fire to do the role of Teresina in *Napoli*. In 1875 she was promoted to solo dancer. The following year she starred in Bournonville's final, and one of his most successful, ballets, *Fra Sibirien til Moskau* (From Siberia to Moscow). Her successor at the Royal Ballet when she retired in 1890 was Valborg Borchsenius, a dancer who was to become as important as her older colleague, Hans Beck, in preserving the "Bournonville School" for future generations.

For Bournonville, in the last decade of his life, there were changes perhaps bigger than those requiring new ballerinas, new danseurs, new contracts, new ballets. For years he had pointed out the inadequacies of the old Royal Theater building, erected in 1748 and, by nineteenth-century theatrical standards, inadequate for the new ballets, the new operas, the new spectacles, the new concepts of staging and decor. June 1, 1874, the old theater, which had housed the history of the two greatest eras in Danish ballet—the Galeotti and the Bournonville—closed. The program that evening included, appropriately, a Bournonville ballet-epilogue called simply *Farvel til det Gamle Theater* (Farewell to the Old Theater). Demolition of the building began almost immediately.

The new Royal Theater, the one that stands today in Kongens Nytorv (New Royal Square), was built adjacent to the old theater. It was much larger in every way, and some of the actors threatened to resign because they said the new stage was "like standing out on a great plain trying to cope." All of the Bournonville ballets had to be redesigned not only with respect to sets and props but also choreographically, since

Ellen Price in *The Sylph*. (From the 1903 motion picture by Peter Elfelt)

Valborg Borchsenius, Ellen Price, Elisabeth Beck, and Anna Agerholm in *Orpheus and Euridice*. (From the 1903 motion picture by Peter Elfelt).

increased stage areas had to be filled effectively. The new theater opened October 15, 1874. The first new work that Bournonville created for the new theater (which today is called the *gamle*, or old) was a Danish-story ballet, *Arcona* (1875). His final work, *From Siberia to Moscow*, came in 1876. He retired the following year, this time permanently, for the two years left to him.

Bournonville had wanted to go to Russia for a long time. Indeed, as far back as the 1830's he had had invitations to

perform there, for the czar had seen him dance in *Valdemar* and had invited him to come to St. Petersburg as a guest artist. He could not accept at that time, but he never lost interest in a visit to Russia. His curiosity about the ballet in St. Petersburg, where his pupil Christian Johansson had become a pedagogical force in Russian ballet, increased with the years. His appetite was whetted even more by articles on Russia that he read in *Revue des Deux Mondes*. He began to take lessons in the Russian language and achieved a usable smattering of the tongue.

Valborg Borchsenius and Hans Beck in *Napoli*.
(From the 1903 motion picture by Peter Elfelt)

He arrived in St. Petersburg (subsequently traveling on to Moscow) in 1875, and was treated as an honored guest not only by Johansson, as was to be expected, but also by the greatest creative force in Russian ballet of that era, Marius Petipa. Petipa had not yet prepared, through choreography and/or conception, such ballets destined for immortality as *The Sleeping Beauty, Swan Lake* or *The Nutcracker,* but his *Don Quixote, Esmeralda* and other ballets popular principally in the last century were the backbone of the Russian Imperial Ballet. He was the undisputed czar of Russian ballet just as Bournonville was the benevolent (usually) despot of Danish dance.

The two geniuses admired each other enormously. During Bournonville's visit they engaged in many frank discussions. Bournonville, the senior of the two, was outspoken in criticism as well as praise, and Petipa, in several instances, agreed with his Danish colleague's less than flattering opinions. For the most part, Bournonville was stimulated by what he saw of Russian ballet, proud of his Johansson and his accomplishments. He found himself inspired by the people and the culture of Russia rather than by ballet performers and glittering technicians.

He reached Russia in the spring in time for carnivals and great activity in the marketplaces, the sort of experience that had excited, rewarded and fed him on his first visit to Italy more than thirty years before. Petipa and Johansson gave a great party in his honor; Petipa presented him an autographed picture with his "hommage" to Bournonville inscribed on it; rehearsals, classes, performances and all kinds of theater events were open to him. Bournonville wrote, "No wonder I see Russia and Russians in a pink cloud BUT I'm not blind to the darker spots."

Among the ballets he attended were *Don Quixote, Esmeralda, Papillon, Le Roi Candule* and *La Fille du Pharaon.* While watching them, he tried to put aside the system and style he had followed for more than forty years. He was both attracted to and amazed by the stage effects and the beautiful decors, and he recognized the advantage of having two hundred dancers, mostly young and beautiful, constantly available for the productions. Nor was he indifferent to the technical skills, the "gymnastic" prowess of the dancers, which he found to be especially remarkable in the girls. But there was a major reservation: "They have not realized that it is the beautiful and the graceful that is the most difficult and the most rare thing in the art of dance. I looked in vain for common sense, logic, beauty, grace."

Bournonville believed, of course, in strong technique, but he believed equally in "concealing difficulty." As for the ballet he saw, "not only was it difficult, it looked difficult. Ballet mustn't be simply a show." He told Petipa that he was impressed with Russian ballet technique, then added what he did not like about the dancing and that he found much of the choreography lacking in dramatic interest and logical development. Both Petipa and Johansson agreed with him. However, they said that since the public and the dancers wanted such displays, they had no choice but to provide what was insisted upon. Since Bournonville himself would never accept the pressures of fashion, he found Petipa's resignation to popular taste difficult to understand. The brilliant but overly gymnastic technique to one side, Bournonville found fault with the dress of the dancers. The new short *tutu*—the Romantic Age length for the tutu was at the calf and the new Russian style was halfway up the thigh—he found "indecent" and commented that the shortness was so exaggerated "they might be good for valkyries who ride horseback but not suitable for court balls, marriages or parties in good company!"

He was even more ferocious and devastating in his remarks about the drawers, or short boxerlike trunks, that the men were required to wear over their tights. These "obligatory" trunks he described as "grotesque fashion." Noting that their use had started in Paris theaters, he deplored the fact that they were now continued, perpetrated and "tastelessly reproduced" abroad. "Steel yourself," he said, "to these repulsive fashions. You'll realize how ridiculous, how absurd they are." He added that wearing them over tights (designed to encase the contours of the dancer's body and not present to establish style or period) was "incongruous," adding that these drawers or little pants were bad imitations of what was worn by "Italian jugglers," encompassing acrobats, gymnasts, mimes and vaudevillians. He described the misuse of these dreadful trunks as "gøgerer"—grotesque. Petipa and Johansson heartily agreed, but shrugged and said that they were worn on orders of the direction.

It is interesting to note that when Nijinsky, decades later, dared to appear without these "drawers," he offended the Dowager Empress to the degree that a scandal ensued and he was suspended from performing at the Imperial Theater. When the Bolshoi Ballet from Moscow and the Kirov (formerly the Maryinsky) Ballet from Leningrad (St. Petersburg) first visited America nearly a century later, the male dancers still

The old Royal Theater in Copenhagen (1748-1874).

wore these presumably modest, overly prudish, unlovely drawers. In subsequent tours and even on home stages in the Soviet Union, the old "gøgerer" fashion began to disappear and is now rarely seen.

The Dowager Empress of Nijinsky's day was a lovely crown princess when Bournonville saw the Danish-born lady in St. Petersburg. Presented to her, he described the occasion: "I stood in front of the same sweet little princess whom I had once taught [a minuet] along with her brothers and sisters. She gave me her hand and talked to me in Danish. She was with her little sons, one of which I suppose will one day become emperor. They jumped around her like little cupids." One of the cupids grew up to be Nicholas II, the last Czar of All the Russias, murdered along with his Imperial Family by revolutionaries in 1918. (The "Little Princess" became the

Today's Royal Theater on Kongens Nytorv (New Royal Square), opened 1874. The old building stood to the right where broad traffic lanes are now in operation.

The Royal Box in the Royal Theater (Det Konglige Teater). Shown here is the late King Frederik IX (himself a Bournonville expert and a conductor of distinction) with Queen Ingrid (left) and the Royal Princesses Margrethe (now Queen Margrethe II), Benedikte and Anne-Marie (now the consort of exiled King Constantine of Greece). The four royal ladies continue their weekly Bournonville classes to this day.

On Bournonville's visit to Russia, another choreographic genius pays homage to his colleague.

Dowager Empress, survived the Russian Revolution and lived out her days in Denmark.)

Bournonville had nothing but praise for the ballet school at the Imperial Theater where Johansson taught. He found the students to be beautifully trained and he commented on the fact that the dancers were well paid by their emperor.

What Bournonville enjoyed most in Russia were the national dances, just as he had in Italy. He was especially impressed with the dances for men as he found them in Russian folklore events. In his book, *My Theater Life*, he describes with gusto his observations in the Moscow marketplace with its carnival atmosphere. "Everyone seemed to be happy. Soldiers, sailors and peasants intermingled and everyone was polite. No strong drinks were offered but there was plenty of tea from steaming samovars. The sounds were almost deafening and combined music of all pitches, the tramping of soldiers' boots, the shouts of hawkers, the voices of men both old and young." He noticed one old man wearing a rope beard who stood on a box and called out to him with smiles and shouts of pure exuberance. "I was so taken aback by his joy that the man apparently thought I understood what he was saying, for he looked at me, smiled at me, jumped down from his platform and into my arms and asked for money!"

In Michel Fokine's great ballet *Petrouchka* (to the famous Stravinsky score), created in 1911, is a carnival scene in a Russian marketplace: soldiers, sailors and peasants—and an old man with a rope beard. Svend Kragh-Jacobsen, today's dean of Danish dance critics, has written how amazing it is that Fokine's *Petrouchka* is what Bournonville described seeing in 1875 in a Moscow market.

While in Russia, Bournonville did not envision a "Petrouchka," but here he found the theme for what was to be his last ballet, *From Siberia to Moscow*. It is the story of a Siberian prisoner who escapes and finds freedom in Sweden. The prisoner in Siberia has a beautiful daughter who plans to help him escape. She enlists the aid of Ivanov, a young Russian officer, and the story reaches a happy conclusion when the czar, impressed with her beauty and her lovely dancing, frees the father. The ballet was richly colored and vibrant with the choreographed evocations of what Bournonville had observed on his journey: the bustling marketplace with its huge cast of differing characters, colorful folk measures and a roaring drunken cossack dance. The ballet was a huge success, and Copenhagen audiences were astonished that such an elderly man could travel to a strange land, absorb so much so quickly and translate his detailed and astute observations into such a vivid work of theater.

A few contemporary Bournonville researchers with leftist views have occasionally tried to prove that Bournonville had socialist leanings and that his trip to Russia and his final ballet proved this interest. True, he did not think well of the absolutism of the czar any more than his father had supported the autocracy of France's pre-Revolution monarchs. But both were

The result of Bournonville's journey to Russia—he was seventy years old—was a rousing ballet which proved to be not merely his last but one of his most spirited and vigorous works, *From Siberia to Moscow*, which may have anticipated such later Russian-rooted masterpieces as Fokine's *Petrouchka*.

clearly loyal and devoted subjects of the kings they served throughout a span of more than a century. So Bournonville's *From Siberia to Moscow* was not the result of socialist inclination but simply a good romantic and dramatic story to tell after being fascinated with Russian folk materials and finding the Russian people in their carnival mood as joyous and vigorous as the people of Italy he had come to love so many years before. No, for all his life August Bournonville was honored to be the king's ballet master.

10

"The Unknown Line Continues"

WITH *From Siberia to Moscow* and Bournonville's retirement as director of the Royal Ballet, chief choreographer and teacher, an era in ballet in Denmark had come to an end. The ephemeral nature of dance itself, plus the fact that the age of motion pictures had not yet arrived and dance scripts were inadequate to record dances for posterity, posed the question, "How long could Bournonville's ballets survive?" Changing tastes in theater and in ballet could also hasten their journey to oblivion. What, then, was the solid stuff of Bournonville dance? All of his ballerinas but one (Maria Westberg, his final discovery)—Kraetzmer, Grahn, Nielsen, Price, Hennings—had become dance history. Their memories, in the case of those who lived long or cared about Bournonville, could be tapped. But the ways in which they had brought Bournonville choreography to life were now merely legend, perhaps merely myth.

There were the male dancers too, several performing long after Bournonville's retirement and even after his death. Their memories were useful, as were those of youthful students with sharp recollections of brief but awesome contacts with the old master. But these memories were fragile and all, because mortality is inescapable, had cutoff dates.

But there were the musical scores for Bournonville's ballets, and they had a notation, universally used musical script that would preserve them forever. Bournonville worked closely with his composers. They were not accompanists; they were artistic collaborators. Because Bournonville actually had a hand in the creation of his ballet scores, his choreographic presence—rhythmically, structurally, dramatically—is preserved in these compositions.

There were six composers who were major in Bournonville's choreographic development. Before their periods of collaboration, the young August worked with Claus Schall, chief composer for Galeotti. Such musicians as Philip Keck and Ludvig Zinck worked chiefly in arranging, rearranging or reworking themes by composers of French ballets. With Frølich, Bournonville had his first major collaborator. Løvenskjold he had brought in from outside the theater to compose *La Sylphide,* but most of his composers were assigned to the Royal Theater and some were actually the rehearsal musicians for the ballets, those working in almost daily duty with Bournonville.

After Frølich, who battled with Bournonville when a failure obscured the preceding successes, and after Løvenskjold, the remaining four composers influential in the Bournonville career were Holger Simon Paulli (composer of Act I and the tarantella in Act III, *Napoli,* plus *Konservatoriet, Kermesse in Bruges, Wedding in Hardanger* among the most famous); Edvard Helsted (*Toreador*); Niels Gade (Act II, *Napoli;* Acts I and III, *A Folk Tale*); J. P. E. Hartmann (*Valkyrie; The Ordeal of Thrym; Arcona;* Act II, *A Folk Tale*); Hans Christian Lumbye (some twenty-five pieces for Bournonville divertissements). (C. C. Møller, a colleague of Lumbye, composed the score for *From Siberia to Moscow.*)

One might think that Bournonville was rather offhand about his musical requirements since more than one composer worked on the same ballet. But the results were by no means patchwork. Bournonville himself had been an accomplished musician since childhood, and during those formative years in Paris he had been exposed to the finest composers of his day. Late in his career, when he staged *Lohengrin* for the Royal Danish Opera (1870), he had not only seen performances of it in Germany but had conducted correspondence with Richard Wagner himself. Wagner was delighted that Bournonville was producing his works in Denmark, and he expressed the hope that the Danes would assume a more

German-oriented production policy in the future. Bournonville, who hated Prussian power threats, replied (in French): "German culture will always be welcome in Denmark; never German politics."

Bournonville, a cultivated artist musically, used composers the way he did because of his sensitivity to each composer's special forte and because he was astute about his own dramatic needs. In most Bournonville ballets, the dramatic element was paramount. For example, in *A Folk Tale* he had Hartmann, a composer of symphony and opera and, for his time, of the avant-garde, compose the witches' music for the second act, while selecting the composer of Mendelssohnian-style romantic music to compose the music for the very Danish folk atmosphere of the opening and closing acts. Gade's wedding music for this ballet is still used today at Danish weddings, as Mendelssohn's wedding music is commonly played in other lands.

The almost family closeness of the performing and the creating artists of the Royal Theater finds a good example in Paulli. At twelve he was a violin pupil with the Royal Orchestra; subsequently he was engaged by the orchestra on a permanent adult basis. Next he served for many years as rehearser with the ballet (what we would today call a "rehearsal pianist"). In 1863 he was promoted to conductor of the opera and given the status of the highest musical authority in the Royal Theater. His career within the Royal Theater environs spanned sixty years. He was an accomplished composer (*Konservatoriet* was a wholly original musical score), but he was specially adept at incorporating folk music themes into the fabric of his own compositions. This he did to brilliant effect in *Kermesse* and in the *Hardanger* ballet. For *Napoli* there is a supposition that Bournonville supplied Paulli with the tune for the tarantella, perhaps remembered from his visit to Italy. But such musical interweavings for the theater often result in major scores of unforgettable beauty—in our day one could point to Aaron Copland's *Appalachian Spring* for Martha Graham.

The musical scores for the great Bournonville ballets survive, along with the composers' notes and instructions (many or most of them derived from Bournonville's stated wishes)

Among Bournonville's most important collaborators were his composers. Because he was a fine musician himself, once urged by the composer Rossini to seek a career in music, he demanded the best of these music masters (clockwise from top left): J. F. Frølich (1806-1860), Hans Christian Lumbye (1810-1874), Edvard Helsted (1816-1900), Niels W. Gade (1817-1890), Herman Løvenskjold (1815-1870), Simon Holger Paulli (1810-1891).

and in many cases with the choreographer's own notes, sketches, diagrams. Not all of them are decipherable today, but many are. Some are in Danish, a few in French. In the Royal Library, which possesses a treasury of Bournonville data of every imaginable sort, a researcher could find a document such as the one describing *Konservatoriet.* On page one, in small, even penmanship: "*Conservatoriet,* Ballet i 2 Akter Notes Choréographiques, Scene Ier: I. Dufour entre par la porte du fond, ouvre son journal. . . ." And on through mimed passages all numbered and the moods and gestures and stage directions clearly described. In the dances, the steps are described in the universal terminology of academic ballet, so that one might find "2 degagés en avant" or "Galoppe des jeunes élèves en ligne" or "promenade autour de la harpe" or details

117

of steps that must be repeated, how, where, in what direction and so on.

Detailed notes by Bournonville—and voluminous they were —the musical scores with their notes and the libretti all served as preservatives of Bournonville ballets. And when memories failed, knowledge of ballet styles and periods and degrees of technical advance could be drawn upon to re-create in form and in spirit, if not in each step and gesture, a "lost" Bournonville work. A major area of loss is that large portion of Bournonville ballet that called not upon music or standard steps to communicate a theme but upon acting. Except for his divertissements, Bournonville works were narrative story-ballets, even dance-dramas. Drama was at the core of his concept of ballet.

Two of Bournonville's great ballerinas became even greater

A senior Hans Beck, a mime of great skill, in *Wedding in Hardanger*. Without Beck, Bournonville might have been lost to future generations of dancers.

actresses, but a reverse procedure was still more common, for Bournonville employed a good many actors in his ballets because they were good mimes. The dancers learned from them and they learned from the dancers in this rewarding example of theatrical reciprocity. Sidsel Jacobsen, an authority on *Valkyrie,* in discussing this innovative but now lost work, writes: "The success of the experiment was entirely dependent on the ability to create a congruous pantomimic language. In creating his mythological ballets as mimed dramas, Bournon-. ville forms a link back to Galeotti in that it was the reproduction of the passions which was of paramount interest rather than the intense cultivation of the virtuosity of the dance, which was characteristic of the Romantic ballet." Bournonville considered the traditional pantomime used again and again in Romantic ballet's mimed scenes trite and comparable to the obviously useful but undramatic sign language of the deaf and dumb. For his own works he sought to achieve "harmonious and rhythmical series of picturesque positions, fetched from nature and the classical models, which must harmonize with character and costume, with nationality and emotions, with time and the person." Such choreographic requirements are much more elusive than a clear command to "glissade jeté, glissade brisé" or the like.

Changing tastes in the theater of ballet did not help in the preservation of Bournonville ballets. Long mime scenes were shortened or deleted. In a related move, the popular plays of Holberg were sometimes edited so that in the post-Bournonville era Holberg plays and erstwhile full-length Bournonville ballets could be given on the same program. Act II of the otherwise perennially popular *Napoli*—the Blue Grotto scene —got to be so boring to twentieth-century audiences that it came to be referred to simply as the "Brønnum Act," since everyone, while it was on, went next door to a café, Brønnum's, for refreshments. By the 1940's the entire act was cut to about six or eight minutes. In the 1960's it was partially restored, but with more dancing than mime. In the late 1970's an even greater portion of it was recast from mimetic action to dance action.

During a similar period in the first half of the twentieth

century, the traditional mime scenes in such Romantic Age ballets as *Giselle* were severely abridged and mimed "soliloquys" of the Petipa era, such as Odette's mimetic description of her history of enchantment, were also condensed. Audiences wanted to get on with the dancing. But by the 1960's a change had occurred in popular taste. Audiences found Odette's gestural tale charming, and when Giselle's mother warned of the dire fate in store for those who dance too much, the public discovered new delight in archaic gesture skillfully done. Danish dancers never lost their dramatic skills; when the fashion for mime returned, they were better prepared than any ballet folk anywhere in the world to speak in "congruous pantomimic language."

There was one person in particular who assisted immeasurably in preserving the art of August Bournonville beyond the ballet master's death, through an era of changing tastes, past the "Brønnum" excuses for escape up to this day when every Bournonville bauble as well as pearl is deemed precious. This man was Hans Beck. That Beck should be preserver as well as ultimate successor was not simply a matter of chronology and comforting logic. The mystical seemed to play its part, for Beck's happy fate appeared to be ordained by a most curious event. Ebbe Mørk, the contemporary dance critic-historian, states it this way: "The unknown line, perhaps inexplicable but very real, continues. If you believe in an aesthetic life, there is no death. We know that when Antoine Bournonville was dying at Fredensborg, he asked his son, August, to dance the *Polka Militaire* for him. An era ended; a new age began, but with that unbroken line. Two days before August Bournonville died, he attended a performance at the Royal Theater. The last dance he ever saw was performed by a very young dancer whom he had seen and liked not long before at his debut. The dance? *Polka Militaire*. The dancer? Hans Beck. With death, there was an artistic birth. The aesthetic line was unbroken."

Years later, in 1944, Beck wrote in his autobiography, *The Life in the Dance:* "The night before my debut, the 27th of November 1879, we danced Bournonville's ballet *Valdemar* for the 150th time. I was there as one of the soldiers. After

the performance we met Mr. and Mrs. Bournonville in the
ballet foyer for speeches, wine and cakes. Ludvig Gade ɪnade
a speech to express the dancers' gratitude, and the master
answered with a fatherly speech to his 'dear children in the
art' and he told them to always keep the banner of idealism
high and to protect beauty and truth. The regisseur Fredstrup
took me by the arm and led me to the master, telling him of

August Bournonville's grave, near his father's.

my debut the following night. Bournonville patted my shoulder
and smiled and said, 'You may be sure I'll come.'

"Friday the 28th of November, I had my debut in a serious
pas de deux with Miss Maria Westberg, who Bournonville a
few years before had asked down from Stockholm to replace
Betty Schnell, now Mrs. Hennings. First they played *Tartuffe*.
Our dance was composed by Bournonville except for one male
solo for which the music and steps were by Gustave Carey and
which was choreographed especially for me. The solo was only

forty-eight measures in waltz rhythm but it was terribly difficult because it consisted of steps that didn't belong to the
Bournonville School.

"The master kept his promise. Thru the hole in the curtain
I saw him sitting in his free seat in the second row, the right
side, the king's side [Beck was speaking in terms of stage
right]. We got enormous applause and [later] a very good critique
in *Dagens Nyheder*. Erik Bøgh wrote, 'Mr. Beck went through
his examination with glory.' Later this pas de deux was incorporated into the first act of the opera *The Dumb Girl of Portici,*
and as late as the season of 1943–1944 it was danced in the
second act garden scene of Bournonville's *Kermesse in Bruges.*
My [debut] performance finished with Bournonville's 'Polka
Militaire,' which is now seen in Bournonville's *The King's
Volunteer Guards on Amager.*"

Hans Beck never studied with Bournonville himself, for
Bournonville stopped teaching adult classes in the spring of
1877 and Beck, at sixteen, went into adult classes that same
summer. But Beck remembered: "We could always hear when
Bournonville walked from his office to the classroom, he was
either singing or playing on his violin very difficult passages
of music." After Bournonville's death, young Beck kept in close
contact with the Bournonville family and especially with
daughter Charlotte, who was convinced that Hans Beck was
the one to continue her father's artistic line.

Two days after August Bournonville saw Hans Beck dance
the *Polka Militaire,* he attended church services. On his way
home, he was stricken and taken to a hospital. A young medical
student recognized him and the hospital staff decorated his
room while they sent for Mrs. Bournonville and the children.
But death soon came to the King's Ballet Master. His last will
and testament for his family was personal, but to his "dear children in art" he had a special bequest: "To all who practice the
laborious study of the dance: regard your art as a link in the
chain of beauty, and an ornament to the stage, and respect
the theater as one of the most glorious manifestations of the
intellectual life of nations."

11

Not "A Transient Memory"

ONE HUNDRED AND SIXTY years ago the fifteen-year-old August Bournonville danced a solo that convinced—if further proof were needed—his father and his king that he possessed more than average talent. The solo was called "A Transient Memory." It has long since been forgotten. Bournonville has not, for he is remembered through ballets, through ballet classroom techniques, through the world stature of the Royal Danish Ballet, through the honorable social status of dancers in Denmark, through voluminous writings (his own and those of his contemporaries and successors), but most important of all, within dancing bodies of every generation. Peter Martins, principal dancer of George Balanchine's New York City Ballet and an ardent Balanchine disciple, was brought up in the Bournonville School in his native Denmark, where he occasionally performs. In 1979 he said in an interview that when performing if he were ill or deeply tired or perhaps even injured, "I can fall back on my Bournonville training—it is always there and it will always see me through."

That training, however, might have disappeared if it had not been for Hans Beck. It was not Bournonville's sudden death that led Beck to begin formulating the Bournonville School. In 1879 there was no need to do so. The Royal Danish Ballet repertory was in fine shape, rehearsed by the master himself. Ludvig Gade, an old and trusted colleague of Bournonville, was the director of the ballet, and Beck himself, a pupil of the virtuoso Danish dancer Ferdinand Hoppe (who had won acclaim at La Scala, where he had partnered Grahn, and who had been one of Bournonville's successors as a dancer) was much too occupied with his ascendant career as a performer. He became a solodancer in 1881 and, like Antoine and August before him, received a government grant that permitted him to study and observe abroad. As the male dancer in Paris almost disappeared from view, Beck was not only retaining but was enhancing the status of the danseur in Copenhagen, adding new roles to his repertory and winning a large public.

But decay was eroding the Bournonville establishment. The government, during one of its recurring fits of economy, was cutting ballet budgets. Gade, lord protector of the Bournonville heritage, retired in 1890. Emil Hansen, the ballet master, became ill and almost incapacitated, and some of the directional duties devolved on the young Beck, a job he did not particularly relish. In 1894 he officially succeeded Hansen as ballet master and head of the Royal Danish Ballet, a position he held for twenty-one years.

Thirty years after Bournonville's death, it became clear to Beck that Bournonville was slipping away. Old dancers were dead or retired, newcomers were learning new ballets, tastes were changing. During the years 1908, 1909 and 1910, Hans Beck formulated and developed the Bournonville School. There were six scheduled classes for the week. Following Bournonville's own teaching method, Beck incorporated dances from Bournonville ballets into this training regimen. This became the established school of the Royal Danish Ballet. Although stage dancing was influenced by the coming of such visitors as Michel Fokine and, briefly, Balanchine, the actual training method of the Bournonville School remained the same until the great teacher, Vera Volkova, joined the Royal Danish Ballet as principal teacher in 1951. One of the weaknesses of the Bournonville School, with its set class for each day of the working week, was that it contained no surprises. Furthermore,

The Bournonville steps, style, lift and lilt . . .

pupils, feigning indisposition, could skip that day containing steps and exercises they disliked or found too difficult.

There was, and is, nothing alien to ballet in the Bournonville School. Following the *barre* work, which each teacher devises with respect to the needs of a specific class, come *adagio* exercises, the *tendu,* the *pirouette, allegro* actions including *batterie,* jumps, leaps, etc. What Beck did was to put together exercises in these categories that Bournonville himself had devised over the years and combined them, as Bournonville had done, with pertinent (to that particular class) excerpts from his ballets. The classroom music Beck assembled was mostly that used by or familiar to Bournonville or, occasionally, later music suitable to support certain exercises. Until 1930 all of this music was played on the violin, for in the old days the ballet master was usually an accomplished violinist who could accompany his pupils and, when necessary, use his bow to flick a careless pupil on arm, leg or body. After 1930 these classroom airs and rhythms were transcribed for piano.

Thus steps, style, movement combinations were preserved

... as demonstrated by the Royal Ballet's ...

by Beck in his creation of the Bournonville School. Preserving the ballets, as discussed earlier, was achieved through memories passed down from generation to generation, through Bournonville's elaborate notes (some bordering on the cryptographic), through musical scores and through descriptive writings. Beck was closely assisted by his younger colleague and frequent partner, Valborg Borchsenius, who was born in 1872 when Bournonville was alive and who served as solo dancer with the Royal Danish Ballet from 1895 until her retirement in 1918. Beck had used Bournonville's notes to his *répititeurs* and was able to unravel a good deal of this shorthand. He passed these notes on to Harald Lander, a Beck pupil and Royal Dancer who became ballet master in 1930. Borchsenius, meanwhile, evolved her own system of notes, which were fairly primitive but are readable and usable. Thus, with all of these elements of recording, it is possible to reconstruct with reasonable accuracy ten or twelve Bournonville ballets.

. . . present senior star, Niels Kehlet.

How does the personal line keep extending? Beck was an adult while the Bournonville ballets were still in a condition approved by the master. Beck guided Borchsenius and Lander. Among Borchsenius's pupils was Gerda Karstens (born 1903), who danced at the Royal Theater for fifty years (she had first appeared at seven as a child dancer). The Karstens name may not be well known outside of Danish ballet circles, for Miss Karstens was not the usual-type ballerina. She was a mime and a great one. Her importance to the Bournonville tradition is of vast significance in the preservation of Bournonville's art, for mime, acting, drama were of primary concern to the master, and none of these aspects was preserved in the Bournonville School. Miss Karstens learned from Beck and

Borchsenius and, after her retirement as a dancer, began to teach mime at the Royal Theater Ballet School, offering (as Borchsenius had before her) the training in mime so important to Bournonville.

Gerda Karstens' farewell in 1956 was an unforgettable event. She played the role of Madge, the witch, in *La Sylphide*, along with the part of the old headmistress in David Lichine's *Graduation Ball*. No ballerina ever received greater applause. King Frederik IX, in the Royal Box, rose to his feet to lead the ovation, and Miss Karstens, making her way through a forest of floral offerings to "the king's side," curtsied to the floor.

Miss Karstens' Madge was one of the great dance portraits of our day. She had started to develop the part when she was still a young woman. Borchsenius was her coach. "She told me," recalled Miss Karstens in the fall of 1978, "to walk like a woman of ninety. I was too young to know how, so I went out to the country and watched old peasant women at work or walking. I picked one who leaned heavily on a stick as my model. I learned the scenes from Borchsenius and the gestures Bournonville had wanted, but my interpretation was my own —that's what Bournonville would have expected. One of the main differences between Bournonville ballets and a good many other ballets of that period was that Bournonville's characters were human. Even Madge was human, despite her magic powers, and to model her walk and movements after a real old woman would have been in keeping with his concepts. Hans Beck didn't help me with Madge—his last year as a teacher was my first as a student—but he approved of what I did with Madge."

Miss Karstens, when assigned the part of Madge, was one of the first women to play the part in many years. "Bournonville," she says today, "preferred the right sex for the right role, but often Madge was turned over to men because the role demands great strength and powerful dynamics. I was able to do it. Borchsenius—she was a bitch!—taught me and Beck supervised and I portrayed and it really worked."

Miss Karstens insists upon the unbroken flow of the dramatic line within a ballet, and she deplores today's permissiveness in the bowing after a solo or duet or scene. "You interrupt

Henning Kronstam—
grand jeté en attitude,
or "a Danish embrace
in air." (*Konservator-
iet.*)

yourself if you acknowledge applause. You can't go down to
the audience, bow and then go back and resume interrupted
love-making!" Her own stage discipline was such that when
playing the mother in *Giselle,* on a given bar of music her eyes
welled with tears.

Of her gallery of characterizations in Bournonville ballets,
she says: "I learned from those who came right before me and
they learned from their predecessors right back to Bournonville's time. I have never changed a scene but I have had
freedom of interpretation within that scene, and that is the
way to keep alive the 'human-ness' that was always Bournonville's goal."

Beck urged Borchsenius to teach "scenes" from Bournonville
ballets to Margrethe Schanne, Mona Vangsaa, Poul Gnatt and
Kirsten Ralov so that they would become accustomed to "play-

Konservatoriet (The Conservatory), created by Bournonville in 1849, was his choreographic reconstruction of a ballet class in Paris of the 1820's as conducted by his teacher, Auguste Vestris. The little blond boy on the right is Nilas Martins, son of one of today's major male dance stars, Peter Martins.

Peter Martins, photographed by Ralph McWilliams (for whom the picture was autographed in later years) in 1958, as he was being instructed by Hans Brenaa, Bournonville expert, under a bust of Bournonville, Royal Theater, Copenhagen.

Konservatoriet. The full view; Ruth Andersen and Solveig Ostergaard as two of the principal girls; from the 1940's, Mona Vangsaa, Kirsten Ralov, Borge Ralov (the dancing master).

ing a scene" as well as dancing Bournonville variations. When Karstens became the mime teacher at the Royal Theater for upcoming dancers, she taught basic mime, traditional scenes, and then, giving each student a piece of music, invited them to create their own dramatic scene. Thus is kept alive the dramatic eloquence of gesture Bournonville demanded of his dancers.

Kirsten Ralov, today associate director of the Royal Danish Ballet, was a pupil of Borchsenius, and the class violinist was a Mr. Andersen. Borchsenius resigned as teacher but returned later as a coach, and she told young Kirsten, "If you know the *school*, then you can tell what is right and what is wrong when you do the Bournonville ballets themselves." When Kirsten graduated, along with her brother, Poul Gnatt, and Schanne and Vangsaa, Hans Beck was present and said to that particular quartet, "You did very well. I think you have a future." His prediction proved correct, for Schanne became the greatest

Wednesday's Class, choreographed by Kirsten Ralov and Fredbjørn Bjørnsson, a contemporary ballet. Just as *Konservatoriet* is Bournonville's remembrance of a Vestris class, so this new ballet is a staging of a long-preserved Bournonville class. Here, Niels Kehlet and Annemarie Dybdal are the featured dancers.

interpreter of the title role in *La Sylphide* for her generation. Gnatt rose to solo dancer rank and then took Bournonville ballets with him to other lands. Vangsaa came to excel in both Bournonville and, later, Balanchine ballets. As for Kirsten Gnatt, whose first husband was the company's premier danseur, Børge Ralov, whose name she took, she became the perfect Bournonville dancer, light, quick, open. She also, through Mme. Borchsenius, became a Bournonville expert; today she is recognized internationally as an authority on Bournonville, theatrically in terms of his ballets and pedagogically with respect to the Bournonville School. In these most important duties she follows in the steps of her senior, Hans Brenaa, who has taught Bournonville classes to generations of Danish children at the Royal Theater and mounted Bournonville choreographies around the world.

Miss Ralov, dedicated to preserving Bournonville but not to mummifying him, realizes that the extended mime of Act II of *Napoli*, the one-time "Brønnum Act," has to be adapted for today's public. In staging a new production for the Royal Ballet in 1976, she choreographed a wholly appropriate ensemble dance for the enchanted maidens of the Blue Grotto using only steps, movements and combinations that Bournonville used elsewhere or that are in the Bournonville School. The mime necessary to the plot was retained and the whole emerged as pure Bournonville, freshly paced.

Ralov is fussy about changes that violate Bournonville structure. "Today's male dancers can do six, seven or more

Margrethe Schanne (with Poul Gnatt) was the unparalleled interpreter of *La Sylphide* for the mid-twentieth century when the Royal Danish Ballet first emerged from Denmark to bring Bournonville to the world.

The Danish *La Sylphide,* since the days
of Lucile Grahn and Bournonville himself, has been a challenge, a delight and
a reward for international ballet stars:
Italy's Paolo Bortoluzzi and Carla Fracci;
Denmark's Mette Hønningen and Flemming Ryberg; . . .

pirouettes, but Bournonville ballets are choreographed, musically, for three turns. You cannot do more without destroying
the phrasing, and no matter how fast the dancer tries to do
them, the preparation for such multiple turns has to be longer
and thus the music is distorted at the beginning as well as at
the end." As for turns in air, Miss Ralov reminds non-Danish
dancers that Bournonville's choreography requires alternate
directions. She knows that some dancers are "left" turners

. . . Denmark's Peter Schaufuss, interna-
tional star, and Anna Laerkesen; . . . Fracci with one of the great male danc
ers of the twentieth century, the world
star from Denmark, Erik Bruhn; . . .

... Hungary's Ivan Nagy, with the American Ballet Theatre; ...

while others are "right." Says Ralov: "No excuses for the men. Pick your favorite side, and when you come to the familiar sets of three turn first to that side, once to the other and back to the first. If you try to do it any other way, you have to sneak in a step and that's wrong."

As for dancing on *pointe*, in Bournonville's first years as ballet master the ballerina could do little but step on to *pointe*, pose and descend. Until the 1950's Danish female dancers did pirouettes on half-toe when it came to Bournonville ballets, as they had done in the era of Lucile Grahn, although they did elaborate toe work in ballets by Fokine, Balanchine and their own Harald Lander. Ralov is by no means insistent on this aspect of authenticity. "Pirouettes on *pointe* for Bournonville are perfectly fine. There is no distortion of phrasing. The girls in Augusta Nielsen's day didn't do much on *pointe* simply because they couldn't in the shoe they wore then. Today's shoes permit such work. Why not do it? But you mustn't fall off *pointe!* Come down smoothly."

139

. . . Flemming Flindt, former director of
the Royal Danish Ballet, in Act I's Scot-
tish dance.

In a "pure" ballet such as *Konservatoriet* (Act I), Ralov says
that small details change with the years. "The steps and port-
de-bras are exactly as they have always been, but with contemporary ballet training in all the dancers' bodies, the preparations for turns and other steps are different. And I notice a
change in stage behavior. In Bournonville, you must be *aware*
of the audience but you must not *play* to that audience. Legs
are trained to go into higher extensions than they used to. It
is very nice, I like it and there is nothing wrong with extending
the *degree* of the lifted leg as long as you don't change or dis-
tort the *way* in which you get the leg to go where you want it
to go."

Harald Lander, onetime director of the Royal Danish Ballet,
and Margot Lander captured
the spirit of Spain in *Far From
Denmark*.

Eskimos, à la Bournon-
ville, as portrayed by
Inge Sand and Niels
Kehlet in *Far From Den-
mark*.

Ralov and her contemporaries were totally trained in the
Bournonville School and were finished dancers when Mme.
Volkova arrived with today's elaborate Russian ballet technique
as originated by Agrippina Vaganova (a pupil of Christian
Johansson) and continuously developed by herself. These
senior dancers studied with Volkova, of course, and extended
their own dance skills under the tutelage of one of the great
teachers of the century. Erik Bruhn, who became the great
premier danseur noble of the 1950's and 1960's, was sufficiently younger to be molded by Volkova. His base was the

Henning Kronstam, the dashing and handsome premier danseur of a few years ago, became a director of the Royal Danish Ballet but continued to perform as a mime, as shown here in a classic comic role in *Napoli*.

Napoli, Act III, in a single performance can give stage home to generations of dancers from the eight-year-olds on the bridge through the junior stars (such as Linda Hindberg) to the great dance mimes of sixty and more years old.

Bournonville School, but the extended virtuosity, the polish were provided by Volkova.

Bruhn at one time admitted that with the new horizons Volkova opened to him and his early experiences with the American Ballet Theatre, he pushed Bournonville to one side, only to "rediscover" him in later years and come to cherish the substance and the spirit of his work. Wrote Bruhn in *Beyond Technique,* "When I think of Bournonville I have to go on from where I see him, and that is from inside me."

And Bournonville, for many dancing Danes, does indeed reside within themselves. Bruhn has said so, Martins said it recently. Henning Kronstam, six years younger than Bruhn, was sixteen when he came under Volkova's care. He and Kirsten Simone, Bournonville trained, were young enough to be fully developed by Volkova, and she guided them to the peak positions in the Royal Danish Ballet. They were secure in their Bournonville, but with her they became brilliant exponents of Fokine, Balanchine, Petipa, Ashton and other non-

Borge Ralov, the first dancer in Danish history to be granted the title "premier danseur," met Bournonville's requirements that the dancer be also the accomplished actor. Here as the fisherman-hero, Gennaro, of *Napoli*.

Mona Vangsaa (mother of today's virtuoso star, Peter Schaufuss) and Fredbjørn Bjørnsson (recently changing from Bournonville virtuoso par excellence to Bournonville mime supreme) in *La Ventana*.

Danish choreographers. Bruhn, since he spent most of his adult career outside Denmark, was not as much a total product of Volkova.

Yet Kronstam, too, in 1978 said: "I have Bournonville in my bones, in my body. At sixteen, a new teacher opens your mind, and that was Volkova. But I was lucky. Not only had I studied Bournonville in my classes as a child, but when I was eighteen, I began dancing leads in Bournonville ballets—*La Sylphide* and *La Ventana*—so you see I had both sides, each complementing the other." Appointed artistic director of the Royal Danish Ballet in 1978, Kronstam as successor to Flemming Flindt set about restoring Bournonville in the classroom and on the stage. "I put back Bournonville classes for children from twelve to sixteen years on a twice-a-week basis. They're going to need it musically and with respect to stamina. In a Petipa variation, for example, you often dance along a diagonal, stop and walk or run lightly back to where you started and commence again. In Bournonville there is no stopping; wherever you go, you dance your way there! As a new director I would have ordinarily worked on reviving and restaging Bournonville, but I've had to move quickly to be ready for the Bournonville centennial with the one hundredth anniversary of his death coming in 1979.

"Restaging Bournonville? Oh, yes, it should be done from time to time. Bournonville himself did it when his ballets were moved from the old, old theater to this one, which was new to him. Theater conditions change, so we must make *new* magic and not try for *old* magic. Besides, all our restagers go back to Bournonville's notes. We stick right with his choreographic patterns, and if he says here 'glissade' and there 'jeté' we hold to it, but if a star soloist looks better with arms 'effacé' instead of 'croisé' I would not object. The corps? No changes permitted!"

Kronstam points out that it is very possible to do the so-called "lost" ballets of Bournonville with the designation "after Bournonville," as is often done with Petipa. Flindt did just this with his popular 1978 production of *Toreador*. Although *Valdemar* was once considered Denmark's national ballet, Kronstam believes that even if it could be reconstructed from notes, it should be left to history, as Bournonville once left

Italy, Bournonville-style, is celebrated in one of the master's most popular ballets, *Napoli*. Peter Schaufuss, who started as a child-dancer on the third act bridge-and-staircase, is now down front as the hero.

The Price Family has served the Danish theater from 1795 to the present. Ellen Price (de Plane) continued the Price skills in celebrating the Bournonville tradition but she also created the title role in Hans Beck's *The Little Mermaid* and it is Ellen, sculpted in bronze, that tourists by the millions visit in the harbor at Copenhagen; with Gustav Uhlendorf in *La Sylphide* and in Bournonville's *Kermesse in Bruges*.

Galeotti's *Romeo and Juliet*, because "it is totally out of style." But to Kronstam, the Bournonville that survives is in style forever.

Peter Schaufuss, the son of Mona Vangsaa, versatile ballerina, and Frank Schaufuss, skilled demi-caractère dancer and briefly an interim artistic director of the Royal Danish Ballet, is one of today's most brilliant dancers. He has risen to international fame outside Denmark and Danish ballet with such companies as the New York City Ballet, the London Festival Ballet, the National Ballet of Canada. But Bournonville is never very far away. "When I put on the kilt for *La Sylphide*," he says, "I feel as comfortable as if I were at home in my own bed. When I dance the *Flower Festival* pas de deux I also feel right at home. And although, at this moment, I've just done my first Gennaro in *Napoli*, I felt as if I belonged. It was home. But of course, I've been at home in *Napoli* almost all my life. I was a little boy on the bridge looking down on all the danc-

ing. Then I was in the corps for the third act; next, a fisherboy in Act I; then to the Pas de Six to the ballabile. For the leading part I was coached by Kirsten [Ralov] and Freddie [Fredbjørn Bjørnsson], I read Bournonville's own words about *Napoli* and other writings by people like Erik Aschengreen.

"I appreciate learning from first hand to second hand, etc., for you'd be lost without these links to the past. You learn through coaching, but from there on you, as an individual, must find your own interpretation. I even feel that I'm already preparing myself to one day pass Bournonville on to someone else. Already I know what's right from wrong, but then I started with THE VIEW FROM THE BRIDGE. When you're brought up with it you don't question it, you've got it."

Schaufuss finds the Bournonville training of value to him outside the Danish orbit. "It enables you to do a lot of things that other dancers with different training can't do as well. For example, it teaches you speed. Balanchine requires speed, but

The pas de deux from *Flower Festival in Genzano* has become in recent years one of the most popular dance duets in the world. Here it is danced by María Elena Llorente and Fernando Jhones from Cuba; Denmark's Peter Martins and America's Merrill Ashley with the New York City Ballet; and, of course, by ballet's superstar, Rudolf Nureyev.

I never have to think about it because it's so ingrown. We Bournonville dancers have faster and more complicated steps than the Russians. When I first came to Balanchine this helped enormously because in a lot of his work the beat is fast with a step to each musical count, and that's pretty much what Bournonville is all about. It isn't just chance that Balanchine seems to like Danish male dancers for his company." (There have been five or six Bournonville-schooled men dancers in the New York City Ballet over the years.)

Reverence for Bournonville never totally disappeared from Denmark during those years of changing tastes and before today's renascence of both his art and his school. But there were grumblings. In 1928, on the occasion of the one hundredth anniversary of Bournonville's first ballet premiere, Betty Hennings was present. She was at the gala and, at seventy-eight, as fragile as a feather, spoke in a clear voice of her master and pedagogue. Edvard Brandes (brother of Georg Brandes, Danish historian and literary critic), critic and founder of the great newspaper *Politiken,* was a trifle churlish

Ballet children who can act as well as dance and mature actor-dancers, some of them dancers who have turned to acting in their older

about Bournonville's art, which he found "too virginal." Bournonville belonged to the romantic era, to the Biedermeier period, and Brandes stood for naturalism, liberalism, positivism. But after grumbling that Bournonville ballet skirts were too long and everything too sweet and too nice, he had to come out and proclaim Bournonville "a genius."

The dancers themselves would not cut off the lifeline to their balletic past. Just as the young Schaufuss turns to Ralov and Bjørnsson and to his mother, Vangsaa, for historic guidelines while retaining his own artistic identity, so it has always been. In 1962, on the occasion of Harald Lander's return to Denmark after years away in Paris, a special program was arranged for him; *La Sylphide* was of course to be a part of it. The dancers went to Ellen Price de Plane, then in her eighties, and asked this great-niece of Juliette and Valdemar Price, this ballerina who had danced Hans Beck's *The Little Mermaid* ballet in 1909 and served as the model for the statue in the harbor, for her guidance. She was sitting down, but with her head, arms and half her body she passed on her knowledge of *La Sylphide* just as she had learned it from Juliette Price when she too was old and, because of the injury that had

years and some who are actors turning to the ballet scene, are essential to such story ballets as *The King's Volunteer Guards on Amager*.

ended her career, confined to a wheelchair. Karen Neiiendam was there for this "rehearsal" with Ellen Price and found it "a great experience, unforgettable."

That Bournonville lives on in the bodies of dancers, in memories and in notes and books as well as in performances of his masterpieces is undisputable. That he now belongs to the world of ballet and not to Danish ballet alone is apparent. But even at a low ebb of his popularity in Denmark, when new artistic forces were at work, when naturalism and positivism battled his purity and romanticism, he was not destructible. Back in 1934, just after Fokine and Balanchine had introduced new ballet viewpoints into Denmark, Kjeld Abell, an artist Balanchine had engaged to design three ballets for him, stood somewhere in the middle of an aesthetic path that seemed headed in one direction but which, obviously, had another direction, from which it had come.

Abell wrote: "Danish ballet spelt and read BOURNONVILLE! Whatever street you choose to walk down, on the plaque is written BOURNONVILLE. Bournonville is an enormous and somehow unhandy monument standing in the middle of today's traffic without paying the slightest attention to the fact that traffic has changed a little within the last years. First, you have an uncontrollable desire to overturn him . . . this is no secret. But it is not that easy. He is not made of plaster, and you get the horrible suspicion that it might be made of marble.

"Next you wonder whether you could remove him secretly, little by little on rollers, just the way they did the City Hall in Randers [a city in Jutland]. Nothing doing. He is heavier than a city hall. In fact, only one thing is left—dynamite! but you don't do it. Not because you don't have the heart to do it but

For more than a century and a half, new generations of Royal Dancers have been groomed to keep Bournonville forever alive in the theater of dance. These Bournonville Danes of 1979, the one hundredth anniversary of Bournonville's death, are, in the back row, Linda Hindberg, Ib Andersen, Sorella Englund, Lise Stripp, Arne Villumsen, and Eva Kloborg; in the center, Annemarie Dybdal and Dinna Bjørn; seated, Frank Andersen and Peter Schaufuss.

simply because every time you see the monument or perceive its outlines, you have to take your hat off to it. The beastly thing about Bournonville is that he actually was, and still is, so very good . . . but you can't stand him!"

In the light of today's late twentieth-century ballet boom or, more pertinent to this book, Bournonville Ballet Boom, the impertinent words of Kjeld Abell seem mostly amusing. Their purpose here lies not merely in the somewhat gleeful irreverence of the terminology but, rather, to remind us that the world of art is not exempt from cyclic change. A half-century ago, Bournonville was at the nadir of his cycle; today he again approaches the zenith he earned and enjoyed in his own lifetime. Why should this be true? Because, in my opinion, Bournonville ballet is at one and the same time unique and universal.

There is a fleetness of step—particularly in the almost bubbling *batterie* highlighting his variations—that the balletomane will find in no other classical ballet school. Yet Bournonville choreographs leisure into this very fleetness, allowing the viewer to savor a pose, to relish a moment of romantic propinquity. In many of the great Russian ballet classics, there are stylized interruptions while the dancer (or dancers) assume starting positions or walk to a designated point of departure. In Bournonville, there are no interruptions—there are pauses for pleasuring the eye. The *port-de-bras* always impresses one as being unusually expansive, for the arms do indeed reach out into space as they define classical positions of beauty and elegance. Yet with this expansiveness, there is no fussiness whatsoever, for the arms move clearly and cleanly to their goals along the dancing arcs of action. And with the slightest of exquisitely etched *épaulement,* the delicacy of a shoulder shift suggests archness, coquetry, shyness.

The dances, the variations, though integral segments of the ballets, lend themselves to excerpting, just as many of Petipa's *pas de deux* serve divertissement programs. This represents Bournonville's mastery of structured movement, and in this area he is a master architect. But it must not be forgotten that Bournonville was also a master dramatist, and to experience his genius at its fullest, one should see a complete ballet, or at least a complete scene, for then one discovers in, say, the mimetic actions of a conniving seller of macaroni, a roistering street musician or a malevolent Madge (the witch) that the arts of dancing and acting become one just as they do in most of the great classical dances of ancient India.

Master architect of movement, master dramatist through movement constitute two-thirds of the genius of August Bournonville. The third aspect of genius? Ah, it is perhaps unique to Bournonville among classical ballet choreographers but of universal impact to viewers of all eras—that is, Bournonville, the master humanist. During the cycle when romanticism was giving way to naturalism or realism, Bournonville ballets were regarded as being too sweet, too pure. But even if his ballets are romantic rather than naturalistic, they are all focused upon the human being, with his foibles, his weaknesses, his fallibility. The characteristics of ridiculousness and greed and evil are not obscured, but they are shared with us in the simplest, most forthright terms—human terms. The brighter side of human behaviour prevails in Bournonville ballets, and why not? But let it be said here and now that this paramount side of Bournonville does not mean that his characters, his situations, the aura of his ballets should be described as "goody-goody." Not at all. But dare I say in these embittered times what Bournonville celebrates? It is the desirable, potential "goodness" of humankind. And this, certainly, is why Bournonville survives and is increasingly adored at the start of the second century after his death, for while he designs wondrous movements and creates delectable dramatic situations, he sees to it that the Bournonville dancer, vaulting upward and surging forward in exuberant testament to the mere act of being alive, is also spreading wide the arms in an invitation to an embrace that says "loving" is inextricable from "living." The poet Wordsworth was writing about rainbows when he penned: "My heart leaps up when I behold. . . ." Those who know Bournonville ballets have no need of rainbows. . . .

Appendix A

Conservatoires

Ballet : 2 Actes

Notes chorégraphiques

Scène 1re

1. Dufour entre par la porte du fond ouvre son journal et s'applaudit de son annonce.

2. Mlle Bonjour le poursuit l'interroge Dufour se retournant brusquement "Laissez-moi".

3. Dufour se promène en se pavanant & en regardant les jambes avec satisfaction.

4. Il ordonne à Mlle B. d'aller chercher le peigne et le miroir. Elle obéit en courant. D. prend une chaise et s'assied au milieu de la scène.

5. Mlle B. lui arrange sa coëffure tandis qu'il poursuit la lecture de son journal. (curiosité de Mlle B)

6. Mlle B s'empare du journal, traverse deux fois la scène, poursuivie par Dufour, et parcourant les colonnes.

7. "Ah, je l'ai trouvé; en voilà de belles Vous offrez votre main, par la voie des journaux!

8. Dufour "Eh bien soit! Je trouverai la beauté et la fortune".

12 ... & embrassement. Ernest & Elisa
Alcan & Victorine se promettent bientôt
une pareille fête.
... aux anciens, un corps de ...
... On se place pour la danse

Final (N° 10)

1 et 2. Signal du Bal. Engagement.

3. Rond général & Ballancé.

4. Gᵉ ⌐, p. ? bq ⌐. Chaîne anglaise &
change de places.

5. Galloppe de côté, tour de main & change
de dames.. — remontez en ⌢

6. Les quatre artistes (de droite) en ligne.
It ballonné, ballonné tour de main.

7. Tutti marche en avant. galloppe en déparant
la colonne.. ___ ; Bis sous les bras
& galloppe générale arrivé aux ailes.

8. Mᵐᵉˢ Raimbaud & Fanny avancent avec la
harpe (au milieu)

9. Fanny danse sa Cachucha.
2 cp. dégagés en avant. 2 cp de côté &
It relevé. — Bis de l'autre côté.

10. Promenade autour de la harpe.

11. 4 Tᵈ bq ⌐. 4 dégagés en place ⌐. Bis
à gauche & une petite pirouette finale.

12. Galoppe des jeunes élèves, en ligne.
13. Formez le double · rond (toute les dames)
14. On se place en quadrilles.
15. Moulinet des dames, tour de main aux cavaliers. Bis.
16. Demi-promenade & demi chaine anglaise Bis.
17. Amenez la danse dans le double rond. Partez à l'opposé et rencontrez-vous.
18. Galoppe générale arrivez en lignes.
19. T. d. G & contretemps en descendant remontez en chassé... Bis
20. Groupe final. ···

Fin.

Den danske Ballets private Pensionsfond.

Beretning og Oversigt.

Februar 1875.

Bi have herved den Ære at fremsende medfølgende Beretning om Pensionsfondens Fremgang og Tilvært, samt Regnskab for Aarets Indtægt og Udgift og det er en sand Glæde for os, som vistnok for alle Ballettens Bethundere at see det bedste Foretagende, efter saa Aars Bestræbelser, at nærme sig det forønstede Maal, nemlig den Grundcapital, hvis Renter i Tiden fulde kunne supplere den tarvelige Alderdomsforsørgelse, som det kongelige Theater muligen vil kunne tjente Ballettens itte pensionsberettigede Personale.

Det kan itte ofte not gjentages at dette Korps, hvis Aand og Dygtighed er almeen aner-tjendt, bestaaende af styrretyve ældre og hngre Medlemmer kun tæller otte med kongelig Ansættelse: (med Net til Pension.) Alle de Øvrige ere udsatte for complet Brødløshed i det Tilfælde at de enten ved Alder, Svagelighed, eller tilstødende Uheld blive uanvendelige for Scenen!

Dengang den danste Stueplads stod umiddelbart under kongelig Bestyttelse blev enhver af dens udøvende Kunstnere efter disse velbestaaede Prøve-Aar fast ansat med forholdsmæssig Pension men fra det Tidspunkt da Theatret blev Statsinstitut, indstræntedes denne Liberalitet til et stedse shntende Mindretal og for Djeblittet virter itte blot det underftottende Personale, men en stor Deel af de for-trinligste Kræfter under de kummerligste Forhold med Hensyn til Blittet paa Fremtiden.

Dette mørke Punkt har staaet de forskjellige, paa hverandre følgende Bestyrelser temmelig tydeligt for Øie, men Ben og Tyve Aar ere forløbne uden at man endnu er kommen til noget Resultat med de projekterede Pensionsplaner; en Saadan hviler for Tiden i Folkethingets Udvalg og venter sin Skjæbne i Forening med Theaterlagen. Den er væsentlig grundet paa disse pro Cent Afdrag af Gagerne og et eventuelt Tilskud af Theaterkassen; det Hele indrettet som en Livrente, den kan blive ret forbeelagtig for de heitlønnede Kunstnere og dem, hvis Bag tilfalde en særdeles lang Tjenestid, men for dem, hvis Præstationer fordre Ungdommelighed og hvis Lønninger, som f. Ex. i Balletcorpset ikke gjennemsnittig overstige 400 Rdlr. Rmt. vil et saadant pro Cent Afdrag kun give en saare ringe Livrente endog efter de reglementerede 25 Aars Tjeneste, og i det Hele vbe de Vaagjælbende 100 Rdlr. aarlig i Alderbomsforsørgelse, efter at de fra Barndommen af, have øvet den tilsyneladende muntre men i Virkeligheden besværlige og ofte farefulde Kunst!

Idet vi fremføre vor dybtfølte Tak til de ædle Velyndere, der hidtil have ydet dette vort Foretagende heimodig og kraftig Bistand, anbefale vi det fremdeles til barm og vedvarende Deeltagelse og bede Alle dem, der i den danske Ballets Fremstillinger have fundet, ikke blot et stemningsfuldt Fest-Element, men en æsthetisk Kunstnydelse, at betænke den Fremtids-Betryggelse og den Opmuntring, der ligger i be Bidrag, der bevilligen tjenkes til ufortrøbne Arbeidere i Musernes Tjeneste og paa det Skjønnes Omraade.

Kjøbenhavn i Februar 1875.

A. Løvenskjold.
Formand.

M. Bing.   A. Bournonville.   G. Brodersen.   A. Fredstrup.

L. Gade.   C. B. Henrichsen.   Holten.   H. Scharff.

159

Bidrag

indkomne siden vor sidste Beretning af 10de Februar 1874.

Eugang for Alle.

Fru Ryan	300 Rd
Grevinde Danners Dødsbo	200 —
Justitsraad Christensen (fra Hobro)	100 —
Lehnsgreve Danneskjold-Samsø	50 —
En ubekjendt Beltynder	30 —
Etatsraadinde Sass	25 —
Sognepræst M. T. Turen	20 —
General Wilster	10 —
	735 Rd

Aarlige Bidrag

H. M. Kongen	100 —
Hds. M. Dronningen	100 —
H. kgl. H. Kronprindsen	50 —
H: H. Prinds Hans	20 —
	270 Rd

Fru Signe Puggaard	100 —
Lehnsgreve Lerche (1874—75)	50 —
Fru Consulinde Bloch (1874—75)	40 —
Kammerherre v. Deurs	30 —
Capitain Ammitzbøll (1874—75)	30 —
Grosserer Ruben	25 —
Capitain, Brygger Jacobsen	25 —
Overkammerherre Oxholm	20 —
Justitsraad Stoltenberg	20 —
Lateris	**620 Rd**

Transport	620 Rd
Particulier M. Levin	20 —
Fru Chr. Schmidt-Phiseldeck	20 —
Kgl. Skuespiller Schram (for 4 Aar)	20 —
Greve W. Knuth (1874—75)	20 —
Conferentsraad Linde	15 —
Conferentsraad Dr. Lund	10 —
Oberst Holten	10 —
Baron Gedalia	10 —
Capitain Bruus	10 —
Etatsraadinde Wulff	10 —
Overretsprocurator Simonsen	10 —
Entrepreneur Larsen	10 —
Høiesterets-Advocat Henrichsen	10 —
Grosserer Starcke	10 —
Brænderieier Willian	10 —
Grosserer L. Salomonsen	10 —
Hofballetmester Bournonville	10 —
Grosserer H. B. Cohen	10 —
Kammerherre A. Løvenskjold	5 —
Kammerherre Sick	5 —
Professor Thornam	5 —
Capitain Sjelle	5 —
Proprietair Schou (til Bartofte)	5 —
Frøken C. Bournonville	5 —
Baletdirigent Gade	5 —
Regisseur Fredstrup	5 —
fhv. Solodandser Hoppe	5 —
fhv. Solodandser Scharff	5 —
	890 Rd

160

Ballets by August Bournonville

1829   *Gratiernes Hyldning* (Acclaim to the Graces). Divertissement. Music, M. E. Caraffa, W. R. v. Gallemberg, and F. Sor.

1829   *Sovngaengersken* (The Night Shadow—La Somnambule). 3 acts based on an older ballet by J. Aumer. Music, F. Herold.

1829   *Soldat og Bonde* (Soldier and Peasant). Pantomimic idyl. Composer and arranger, P. L. Keck.

1830   *Hertugen af Vendômes Pager* (Les Pages du Duc de Vendôme). Pantomimic ballet. Music, A. Gyrowetz.

1830   *Paul og Virginie* (Paul and Virginia). Pantomimic ballet. Music, R. Kreutzer.

1831   *Victors Bryllup eller Faedrene-Arnen (Fortsaettelse af "Soldat og Bonde")* (Victor's Wedding, or The Ancestral House—a sequel to "Soldier and Peasant") 1 act. Music, P. L. Keck.

1832   *Faust.* Romantic ballet in 3 acts. Composer and arranger, P. L. Keck.

1833   *Veteranen eller det Gaestfrie Tag* (The Veteran or The Hospitable House). Idyllic ballet in 1 act. Music, L. Zinck.

1833   *Romeo og Giulietta* (Romeo and Juliet). Tragic ballet in 5 acts. Music, C. Schall.

1834   *Nina eller den Vanvittige af Kaerlighed* (Nina, ou La Folle par amour). Pantomimic ballet in 2 acts. Music, L. de Persuis.

1835   *Tyrolerne* (The Tyroleans). Idyllic ballet in 1 act. Music, J. F. Frøhlich (and Rossini).

1835   *Valdemar.* Romantic ballet in 4 acts. Music, J. F. Frølich.

1836   *Sylfiden* (La Sylphide). Romantic ballet in 2 acts. Music, H. Løvenskjold.

1837   *Don Quixote ved Camachos Bryllup* (Don Quixote at Camacho's Wedding). Pantomimic ballet in 3 acts. Arranger, L. Zinck.

1838   *Herthas Offer* (Hertha's Offering). Divertissement. Arranger, J. F. Frøhlich.

1838   *Fantasiens ø eller fra Kinas Kyst* (Isle of Phantasy). Romantic ballet in 2 acts and a final tableau. Music by various composers.

1839   *Festen i Albano* (The Festival in Albano). Idyllic ballet in 1 act. Music, J. F. Frøhlich.

1840   *Faedrelandets Muser* (National Muses). Pantomimic prologue. Composers and arrangers, J. F. Frøhlich and N. W. Gade.

1840   *Toreadoren* (The Toreador). Idyllic ballet in 2 acts. Composer and arranger, E. Helsted.

1842   *Napoli eller Fiskeren og Hans Brud* (Naples or The Fisherman and His Bride). Romantic ballet in 3 acts. Music, H. S. Paulli, E. Helsted, N. W. Gade, and H. C. Lumbye.

1842   *Polka Militaire.* Divertissement. Music, H. C. Lumbye.

1843   *Erik Menveds Barndom* (The Childhood of Erik Menved). Romantic ballet in 4 acts. Music, J. F. Frøhlich.

1844   *Bellman eller Polskdansen paa Grönalund* (Bellman or The Dance at Gronalund). Ballet-vaudeville in 1 act. Arranger, H. S. Paulli.

1844   *En Børnefest* (Children's Party). Divertissement. Composer and arranger, H. S. Paulli.

1844   *Hamburger Dans.* Pas de deux. Music, H. C. Lumbye.

1845   *Kirsten Piil eller To Midsommerfester* (Dirsten Piil, or Two Mid-Summer Festivals). Romantic ballet in 3 acts. Music, E. Helsted.

1845   *Rafael.* Romantic ballet in 3 tableaux (3 acts). Music, J. F. Frøhlich.

1846   *Polacca Guerriera.* Divertissement. Pas de deux. Music, H. C. Lumbye.

1847   *Den Nye Penelope eller Foraarsfesten i Athenen* (The New Penelope, or Spring Festival in Athens). Ballet in 2 acts. Music, H. Løvenskjold.

1847   *Maritana.* Romantisk dansescene. Music, H. C. Lumbye.

1847   *Den Hvide Rose eller Sommeren i Bretagne* (The White Rose, or Summer in Brittany). Ballet in 1 act. Composer and arranger, H. S. Paulli.

1848   *Søndags Echo: Amagerdands* (Echo of Sunday: An Amager Dance). Arranger, H. S. Paulli.

1848   *Gamle Minder eller en Laterna Magica* (Old Memories, or The Magic Lantern). Ballet in 1 act. Arranger, E. Helsted.

1849   *Konservatoriet eller et Avisfrieri* (The Dancing School, or A Proposal by Advertising). Vaudeville-ballet in 2 acts. Composer and arranger, H. S. Paulli.

1850   *De Uimodstaaelige* (The Irresistible). Divertissement. Music, H. C. Lumbye.

1850   *Psyche.* Ballet in 1 act. Composer and arranger, E. Helsted.

1851   *Kermessen i Brugge eller de Tre Gaver* (The Kermesse in Bruges, or The Three Gifts). Romantic ballet in 3 acts. Arranger and composer, H. S. Paulli.

1852   *Zulma eller Krystalpaladset* (Zulma or the Crystal Palace in London). Ballet in 3 acts. Composer and arranger, H. S. Paulli.

1853   *Brudefaerden i Hardanger* (Wedding in Hardanger). Ballet in 2 acts. Composer and arranger, H. S. Paulli.

1854   *Et Folkesagn* (A Folk Tale). Ballet in 3 acts. Music N. W. Gade and J. P. E. Hartmann.

1854   *La Ventana*. Divertissement. Music, H. C. Lumbye.

1855   *Abdallah*. Ballet in 3 acts. Music, H. S. Paulli.

1856   *Den Alvorlige Pige* (The Serious Maiden). Divertissement. Music, A. F. Lincke.

1857   *I Karpatherne* (In the Carpathians). Ballet in 3 acts. Music, H. S. Paulli.

1858   *Blomsterfesten i Genzano* (Flower-festival in Genzano). Ballet in 1 act. Music, E. Helsted and H. S. Paulli.

1859   *Fjeldstuen eller Tyve Aar* (The Mountain Hut, or Twenty Years). Ballet in 2 acts. Music, A. Winding and E. Hartmann.

1860   *Fjernt fra Danmark eller et Costumebal Ombord* (Far from Denmark, or A Costume Ball On Board). Vaudeville-ballet in 2 acts. Music by various composers.

1861   *Valkyrien* (The Valkyrie). Ballet in 4 acts. Music, J. P. E. Hartmann.

1866   *Pontemolle: et Kunstnergilde i Rom* (Pontemolle, An Artist's Party in Rome). Vaudeville-ballet in 2 tableaux. Music, W. Holm, A. F. Lincke, and F. Neruda.

1868   *Thrymskviden* (The Legend of Thrym). Ballet in 4 acts. Music, J. P. E. Hartmann.

1870   *Cort Adeler i Venedig* (Cort Adler in Venice). Ballet in 3 acts and a final tableau. Music, P. Heise.

1870   *Bouquet Royal*. Divertissement. Composer and arranger, H. C. Lumbye.

1871   *Livjaegerne paa Amager* (The King's Voluntary Corps at Amager). Vaudeville-ballet in 1 act. Composer and arranger, W. Holm.

1871   *Udfaldet i Classens Have* (The Sally from the Classen-Park). Tableau arranged after a painting by C. W. Eckersberg.

1871   *Et Eventyr i Billeder* (A Fairy Tale in Pictures). Ballet in 3 acts. Composer and arranger, W. Holm.

1873   *Mandarinens Døtre* (The Daughters of the Mandarin). Ballet-divertissement. Composer and arranger, W. Holm.

1874   *Weyses Minde* (Weyse in Memoriam). Epilogue with tableaux. Arranger, W. Holm.

1874   *Farvel til det Gamle Theater* (Farewell to the Old Theater). Ballet-epilogue. Music, various composers.

1875   *Arcona*. Ballet in 4 acts. Music, J. P. E. Hartmann.

1875   *Fra det Forrige Aarhundrede* (From the Last Century). Ballet-divertissement. Arranger, W. Holm.

1876   *Fra Siberien til Moskau* (From Siberia to Moscow). Ballet in 2 acts. Music, C. C. Møller.

The Royal Danish Ballet in Films
1902–1906

.

The Royal Danish Ballet 1902–1906, motion pictures by Danish court photographer Peter Elfelt, featuring members of the Royal Danish Ballet.
1. Reel from *The King's Voluntary Corps at Amager.* Choreography by August Bournonville (1871). Music by W. Holm. Danced by Valborg Borchsenius, Hans Beck, Ellen Price. Filmed 1906.
2. Children's Dance from *The Elf-Hill.* Choreography by Poul Funck (1828). Music by Frederik Kulau. Danced by Helga Smith, Gudrun Christensen. Filmed 1902.
3. The Sylph's Opening Solo from *La Sylphide.* Choreography by August Bournonville (1836). Music by Herman Løvenskjold. Danced by Ellen Price. Filmed 1906.
4. The Sylph's Opening Solo from *La Sylphide* (longer version). Choreography by August Bournonville (1836). Music by Herman Løvenskjold. Danced by Ellen Price. Filmed 1906.
5. Portions of the Tarantella from *Napoli.* Choreography by August Bournonville (1842). Music by Holger Simon Paulli. Danced by Valborg Borchsenius, Hans Beck. Filmed 1903.
6. Gypsy Dance from *Il Trovatore.* Choreography by August Bournonville (1865). Music by Giuseppe Verdi. Danced by Valborg Borchsenius. Filmed 1906.
7. "Pas de deux." Choreographer unknown. Music unknown (music used: excerpt from Act I of *Flower Festival of Genzano* by Edvard Helsted). Danced by Clara Rasmussen, Margrethe Andersen. Filmed 1902.
8. Jockey Dance from *From Siberia to Moscow.* Choreography by August Bournonville (1876). Music by C. C. Møller. Danced by Gustav Uhlendorff, Richard Jensen. Filmed 1905.
9. Ballet from *Orpheus and Euridice.* Choreography by Hans Beck (1896). Music by Christoph Willibald Bluck. Danced by Valborg Borchsenius, Ellen Price, Elisabeth Beck, Anna Agerholm. Filmed 1906.

Production credits

Music arranged and performed by Elvi Henriksen.
Choreographic consultant: Niels Bjorn Larsen.
Produced by John Mueller and Ole Brage.
A joint production of the Historical Archive of Danish Radio and Dance Film Archive of the University of Rochester.

Films made available by Danish Broadcasting Corporation and the Danish National Museum.
The processing of these films and the addition of sound was made possible, in part, by a grant from the National Endowment for the Humanities.
16mm., 14 min., b/w, sound.
Available for rental and purchase from: Dance Film Archive, University of Rochester, Rochester, New York 14627.

Bibliography

Andersen, Hans Christian. *The Fairy Tale of My Life.* New York: Paddington Press Ltd. (1868 edition), 1975.

Ashengreen, Erik; Bech, Viben; Fridericia, Allan; Jacobsen, Sidsel; Kragh-Jacobsen, Svend; Schiørring, Nils. *Theatre Research Studies II.* Copenhagen: The Institute for Theatre Research, The University of Copenhagen, 1972.

Bournonville, August. *Etudes Choréographiques.* Copenhagen: Chez F. S. Muhle, 1861.

———. *Lettres à la Maison de son Enfance.* Volumes I, II, and III. Copenhagen: The Society for the Study of Danish Language and Literature, 1969, 1970, 1978.

———. *Mit Theaterliv (My Theatre Life).* Kjørenhavn: Forlagt Af Universitetsboghandler, C. A. Reitzel, 1848; C. A. Reitzelforlag, 1877.

Bruhn, Erik and Moore, Lillian. *Bournonville and Ballet Technique.* London: A. & C. Black, Ltd., 1961.

Chujoy, Anatole and Manchester, P. W. *The Dance Encyclopedia.* New York: Simon and Schuster, 1967.

Fog, Dan. *The Royal Danish Ballet, 1760–1958 and August Bournonville, A Chronological Catalogue.* Copenhagen: Dan Fog, 1961.

Guest, Ivor. *Le Ballet de l'Opéra de Paris.* Paris: Théâtre National de l'Opéra, 1976.

———. *The Romantic Ballet in England.* London: B. T. Batsford Ltd., 1948.

Henriques, Alf. *The Royal Theatre, Past and Present.* Copenhagen: Krohns Office, 1967.

Kappel, Vagn. *Contemporary Danish Composers.* Copenhagen: The Danish Society, 1950.

Koegler, Horst. *The Concise Oxford Dictionary of Ballet.* London: Oxford University Press, 1977.

Kragh-Jacobsen, Svend. *August Bournonville, Hvad Bør Danmark Gjøre For Sine Invalide Krigere?* Copenhagen: Strandsbergs Kulturhistoriska Bibliothek, 1978.

———. *The Royal Danish Ballet, An Old Tradition and a Living Present.* London: Adam & Charles Black, 1955.

———. *20 Solodancers of the Royal Danish Ballet.* Copenhagen: Mogens van Haven, 1965.

Kragh-Jacobsen, Svend and Krogh, Torben. *Den Kongelige Danske Ballet.* Copenhagen: Selskabet Til Udgivelse Af.

Leicht, Georg and Haller, Marianne. *Det Kongelige Teaters Repertoire, 1889–1975.* Copenhagen: Bibliotekscentralens, 1977.

167

Moore, Lillian. *Bournonville's London Spring.* New York: The New York Public Library, 1965.

Neilsen, Kay. *Danmarks Konger og Dronninger.* Copenhagen: Vorlaget Hamlet, 1978.

Ralov, Kirsten, ed. *The Bournonville School.* 4 vols. New York: Marcel Dekker, 1979.

Van Haven, Mogens. *The Royal Danish Ballet.* Copenhagen: J. Chr. Sorensen, 1961.

Sitwell, Sachaverell. *The Romantic Ballet.* London: B. T. Batsford Ltd., 1948.

Terry, Walter. *Ballet Guide.* New York: Dodd, Mead, 1976; Popular Library, 1977.

———. *Great Male Dancers of the Ballet.* New York: Doubleday, 1978.

Veale, Tom G. "The Dancing Prices of Denmark," in *Dance Perspectives,* No. 11, Summer 1961.

Wilson, G. B. L. *A Dictionary of Ballet.* London: Adam & Charles Black, 1974.

Winter, Marian Hannah. *The Pre-Romantic Ballet.* New York: Dance Horizons, 1975.

Index